Albert E. Winship

Methods and Principles in Bible Study

and Sunday school teaching

Albert E. Winship

Methods and Principles in Bible Study
and Sunday school teaching

ISBN/EAN: 9783337170417

Printed in Europe, USA, Canada, Australia, Japan

Cover: Foto ©Lupo / pixelio.de

More available books at **www.hansebooks.com**

METHODS AND PRINCIPLES

IN

BIBLE STUDY

AND

SUNDAY-SCHOOL TEACHING

BY

REV. A. E. WINSHIP

BOSTON
W. A. WILDE & CO., PUBLISHERS
25 BROMFIELD STREET
1885

Copyright,
By A. E. Winship.
1885.

To Her

WHOSE METHODS AND PRINCIPLES IN TRAINING AND TEACHING
OUR CHILDREN IN THE HOME HAVE TAUGHT
ME MORE PSYCHOLOGY THAN
ALL MY BOOKS,

I DEDICATE THIS FIRST WAIF FROM
MY PEN.

PREFACE.

No departure from accepted metaphysical science is attempted. The aim is to apply the latest and best matured psychological principles to the training of the intellect, emotions, and will through a reverent study of the Scriptures; to present methods of developing the mind at different periods; to aid in securing attention; to assist the memory and imagination; to develop correct habits in thought and life; to inspire an intelligent belief; to aid in making right choices.

In a few instances the author has recast illustrations that he had previously used editorially in the *American Teacher*, and would acknowledge his appreciation of, and indebtedness to, Sully's *Sensations and Intuitions*; Bain's *Emotions and the Will*; Sully's *Outlines of Psychology*; Hamilton's *Metaphysics*; Bain's *Senses and Intellect*; Carpenter's *Mental Physiology*; Bain's *Mind and Body*; Calderwood's *Relation of Mind to Body*; Jevons's *Logic*.

CONTENTS.

INTRODUCTION.

PAGE

Prominence of Sunday-school Work — The Bible the Text-Book — What, How, and Why? — Popularizing Psychology — Mission of the Sunday-school — International Lessons — No Spirit of Criticism 13

CHAPTER I.
MENTAL DEVELOPMENT.

AIM 19
    Drawing Straight line — Starting a Tune — Teacher's Responsibility — He needs the Key-note.

PRINCIPLES 20
    Knowledge of the Nature and Activity of the Child's Mind — What is to be attained — What is Mental Growth? — Mental Development — Secular Education — Skill in Mechanics, Arts, etc. — Exercise of the Mind — Requirements of Christian Living — Art and Philosophy — Thinking, Feeling, and Choosing — The Bee — Mental Development not necessarily a Blessing — Ingersoll — Moody — Character Development — Memory Age — Inquisitive Age — Analytical Age.

MEMORY AGE 23
    Individual Texts — Care in Selection — Adaptation — Verses or Paragraphs — Point their own Lessons — Rhythmical — Secret Art — The Foundation — Repetition — Verbal Memory — Relish for memorizing Scripture — Too early Development — The Strawberry — Revision Committee — Texts germinate Thought — Drudgery — Teach the Truth — Self-evident Application — Truth harnessed to Real Life — Life fashioned by Truth — Silk-worm — Ruskin's Texts.

INQUISITIVE AGE 28
    Circumstances and Associations — Geography — Cyclamen.

ANALYTICAL AGE 30
    Grouping Texts — Mortified at Ignorance — Will not ask Questions — Home — Mother — Sunday-school — Parental Authority — Biographical Grouping — Abraham — Temperance — General Outline — Fragrant Flowers — Weeds — Relation to Parents — To Children — To Friends — Enemies — Musical Development.

CHAPTER II.
ART OF THINKING.

INTRODUCTION 45
    Experience — Thought in Bible Study — John Jasper — Loyalty to Intellectual Leader — Soldier — Contentment.

  I. APPRECIATION OF SINGLE TRUTHS . . . 48
    1. Of Things Present.
    2. Of Things Present through the Memories.
    3. Of Things Present through the Imagination.
    4. Of Things Absent.

 II. DISCRIMINATION TO NOTE DIFFERENCES . 51
    1. Both Present.
    2. One Absent.

III. COMPARING FACTS TO NOTE RESEMBLANCES . 55

IV. ESTIMATING CONSEQUENCES 57
    Theory in Practice — Patent Office — Physicians — Lawyers — Spider — Benefit of Truth — A Story — False and True Methods of Application — Rule.

 V. INDUCTIVE REASONING 61
    Definition — Examples — Rules.

VI. DEDUCTIVE REASONING 63
    The Art — Principles — Laws — Explanations — Each Law examined — Examples — Adaptation to Age.

CHAPTER III.
ATTENTION.

INTRODUCTION 75
    Object of Mental Discipline — The Magnetic Teacher.

CONTENTS. 9

1. INVOLUNTARY ATTENTION . . 76
   1. Non-attention.
      How not to attend — Humming-bird.
   2. External.
      a. Interested through Senses . 77
         Beaver.
      b. Through Senses, disinterestedly . 78
         Eagle — Sir William Hamilton.
      c. Abstract Attention without Objects present . 78
      d. Application to the Bible 79
         1. Learning Texts because of Rhythm.
         2. Because of Truth we need.
         3. To learn Higher Truths.
      e. Results.
         Control of Circumstances — Men who influence us — Humming-bird.
      f. Methods 81
         Appeal to the Eye and Ear — Familiar in Unfamiliar Surroundings — Question with Animation — Vivid and Suggestive Questions — Teacher must master the Class — Above the Self, above the Teacher to the Truth — Coleridge.
      g. Adaptation to Age 84
         In Secular Schools — In Sunday-schools — Melody — From Eight to Fifteen.
   3. Internal 84
      At Fifteen — Telescope — Mind educated.
II. VOLUNTARY ATTENTION 85
III. INVOLUNTARY OR AUTOMATIC ATTENTION . . 85

CHAPTER IV.
ART OF REMEMBERING.

INTRODUCTION 91
METHODS OF LEARNING TO REMEMBER . . . 91
   Definitely learned — Accurately learned — Firmly fixed in the Mind — Closely associated — Good Mental Attitude.
RECALLING PAST KNOWLEDGE 94
   Involuntary.
      Panorama — Natural Elasticity — Ladies' Satchel — Science of not forgetting Association — Success in Sunday-school Teaching — Keen Attention — Frequent Repetition.
   Voluntary.
      Apply to the Bible — Teacher's Responsibility.

OBJECTS OF MEMORIZING 99
   Words. *i. e.*, texts, chapters, etc.
   Truth without words.
     Parables — Incidents — Miracles — Fish taking air.
   Truth without incident.

CHAPTER V.
PHILOSOPHY OF HABIT.

INTRODUCTION 107
   Bad Habits destructive — Good Habits conserve Mental Energy — Righting Physical Deformities — Good Habits right Mental Deformities.
SUSCEPTIBILITY OF MIND 108
   Body Organism of Growth — Mind of Development.
HABIT AND WILL 108
CONDITIONS OF HABIT 109
   Creates Brain Power — Ice-cutting.
METHOD OF FORMING HABITS 109
   Early Rising — Intemperance — Physical Reforms through Habit — Change of Attention Important — A Shrewd Mother — Current of Thought changed.
HABITUAL INDIFFERENCE 113
HABIT IN MORALITY 114
HABIT IN RELIGION 115
FORMATION OF HABIT 116
   Definite Beginning — Frequent Repetition — Uniformity of Action.

CHAPTER VI.
USE OF IMAGINATION.

INFLUENCE OF IMAGINATION 121
   Properly developed — Keeps from Mischief — Develops Virtue and Faith.
NEGLECT OF IMAGINATION 123
DEVELOPMENT OF IMAGINATION 124

CHAPTER VII.
THE EMOTIONS.

CLASSES OF FEELINGS 131
INFLUENCE OF EMOTIONS 132

PLEASURABLE EMOTIONS	143
PAINFUL EMOTIONS	134
UNSTIMULATED EMOTIONS	135
EXCESSIVE EMOTIONAL NATURES	135
ERRATIC EMOTIONAL NATURES	135
DEVELOPMENT OF EMOTIONS	137
INFLUENCE OF THE WORD OF GOD	140

CHAPTER VIII.
PHILOSOPHY OF SYMPATHY.

IMPORTANCE OF SYMPATHY	145
PHYSICAL SYMPATHY	145
INTELLECTUAL SYMPATHY	146
EMOTIONAL SYMPATHY	147
SYMPATHY OF WILL	148
SYMPATHY, GOOD AND BAD	148
SYMPATHY IN AMUSEMENTS	148
SYMPATHY IN CHURCH	152
INTELLECTUALITY	156
SENSE INFLUENCES	156
HINDRANCES	156

CHAPTER IX.
PHILOSOPHY OF BELIEF.

INTRODUCTION	163
BELIEF	164
DOUBT	168
UNBELIEF	170
DISBELIEF	171
DESPONDENCY	171
DESPAIR	171
DESPERATION	172
BELIEF	174
CREDULITY	175
SUPERSTITION	175
FANATICISM	175
EXPECTANT ATTENTION	177

BELIEF	181
EXPECTANCY	181
RELIANCE	181
FAITH	182
HOPE	182
PEACE	183
JOY	183
CHARACTER OF BELIEF	184
VARIETIES OF BELIEF	186
ADAPTATION OF BELIEF	186
CONFESSION	188
FAITH IN ACTION	189
MOTIVES OF BELIEF	190
INFLUENCE OF THE BIBLE	192

CHAPTER X.
ART OF CHOOSING.

INTRODUCTION	201
CHOICE.	
INVOLUNTARY	201
IMPULSIVE	201
CIRCUMSTANTIAL	201
IMITATIVE	202
VOLUNTARY	204
DELIBERATION	205
DECISION	206
DETERMINATION	208
RESOLUTION	209
MAJOR AND MINOR CHOICES	212
MOTIVES	214
WISH	215
DESIRE	215
COVETOUSNESS	215
PRESENT	216
FUTURE	216
TO PLEASE SELF	218
TO BENEFIT OTHERS	218
TO PLEASE GOD	219
SPECIAL DIVINE ENLIGHTENMENT	220

INTRODUCTION.

THE patriotic, social, and religious importance of the work attempted by the Christian men and women who distinguish themselves from other laborers in the Master's service by emphasizing Bible teaching in the Sunday-school, makes it certain that they will come into greater prominence as the fruit of their labor appears.

The Bible is the text-book of all ages in morals and religion, and upon its truths rest the justice and mercy of human law; the stability of government, the permanency of commercial enterprise, the sanctity of the laws, the honor of man, the virtue of woman, the authority of the Sabbath, the precedent for Divine worship, the merit of the sacraments, the comfort of the afflicted, the consolation of the bereaved, the hope, peace, and joy of mankind.

In teaching this book successfully we must know what to do, how to do it, and why. By a variety of means, through type and voice, we have been aided in teaching the individual lessons with a thoroughness that we have no disposition to criticise. But the great underlying principles of mental action upon which success depends have not been emphasized, reliance having been placed upon the *how* rather than the *why*, upon the indications of immature experiment and experience rather than upon the philosophy which has commanded the respect of the best intellect of all ages. Hence the demand for popularizing those feaures of psychology upon which ultimate success in Sunday-school teaching must depend. The child is not taught effectively until he thinks, feels, and wills habitually within the lines, under the laws, and from the inspiration which God has given in the Bible and conscience.

If at times we shall seem to criticise existing plans and methods it will not be intentional. The uniformity of Bible study under the International system has been too great a blessing to the world to be lightly esteemed, and the system is too dear to the hearts of the multitude who have profited by it to make it wise or courteous to comment with light and easy grace upon those defects that begin to appear as we reach a higher plane. We may well question whether we should have been qualified to see the better way but for the light radiated by the International lessons.

Those who indulge in panegyrics on the glorious old days when the Bible was committed to memory by the chapter, and call for a return to those favored methods, ought to know that the effectiveness of the present system is to that of former days as the dawn to the midnight, and if there is to be improvement it must be in advance and not in retreat. The purpose of this work is to present principles by which we should be guided, and indicate methods of application. It is not our aim to defend or antagonize existing systems.

The leaders, official and otherwise, who have furnished the impetus and developed the wisdom by which present attainments have been gained, and the teachers who have, through self-denial and devotion, made present success possible, have earned the respect and won the regard of all friends of humanity to such an extent that we have neither the intention nor the desire to utter one criticism upon their spirit or methods. Let no word of ours be so construed.

MENTAL DEVELOPMENT.

"Our pleasures and our discontents
Are rounds by which we may ascend."
— LONGFELLOW.

"Each mind has its own method." — EMERSON.

"Grow in grace, and in the knowledge of our Lord and Saviour Jesus Christ." — 2 PET. 3 : 18.

"Nature never stands still, nor souls neither; they ever go up or go down." — JULIA C. R. DORR.

"Notwithstanding a faculty be born with us, there are several methods for cultivating and improving it." — ADDISON.

METHODS AND PRINCIPLES.

CHAPTER I.

MENTAL DEVELOPMENT.

 MAN with an artistic instinct does not draw a straight line hesitatingly, for that makes it rough and uneven. Neither does he strike it off thoughtlessly at a single stroke, for that would curve or wave it. He makes two limiting points, then runs his eye from one to the other to fix the direction, and with a single movement makes a line as straight as an arrow.

The more perfect one's musical skill, the more careful is he never to sound a note until he has the key and has mentally caught the melody of the chord.

The Sunday-school teacher has entrusted to his care the mental, moral, and spiritual development of immortal beings. The way he attempts to teach indicates his comprehension of the responsibilities involved, and appreciation of the methods and principles to be employed. He should know what he has to deal with, and what he must accomplish. The teacher needs the key note and the chord as much as the musician.

The first thing, therefore, is to consider the principles of mental development. There must be knowledge of the child's mind in its nature and activity. There must be, also, a distinct knowledge of what is to be attained by training the mind through the study of the Scriptures.

There is an important psychological distinction between mental growth and development; the former being gradual increase in amount and improvement in quality of knowledge, while the latter is the elaboration of the materials acquired in growth and increase of facility and power to use knowledge. Secular education has often brought itself into disrepute by giving undue attention to the amount of knowledge attained and retained. The Sunday-school has too generally tended in the same direction. Those who have moulded and controlled the world in mechanics and arts, in commerce and war, in literature and religion, have been those who have become skilful in using knowledge with greatest readiness, wisdom, and force. They have acquired the art of training the mind through every exercise for greater accomplishment with the same exertion, or the same result with less effort.

· Christian living requires that the mind develop ability to think, feel, and choose promptly and effectively by applying the truth learned in the practical affairs of life. The aim of the Sunday-school should be to teach the art and philosophy of moulding the thought, feeling, and choice of daily life according to the Divine will as expressed in conscience and Scripture.

The bee stings with painful poison, or delights with honey, according to the application made of nectar taken from the flowers.

Mental development is not necessarily a blessing to the world. It poisons or sweetens according to the use made of the power developed. An Ingersoll poisons the world at a thousand dollars a night, a Moody helps the poor, depressed, conscience-stricken sinner nearer God. Each has studied with care the art of influencing the mind and heart of man.

Mental development is of such a nature that it needs to have character development go hand in hand with it, and there is no line of study or instruction that offers such advantages as the Word of God.

In the unfolding of mind and character through Bible study there are three distinctions that may be clearly made, based on the nature of the human mind, on the changes involved in its unfolding at different periods, on the peculiar adaptations of the various phases of Scripture.

In teaching the Bible there should be an appreciation of three great natural characteristics of children as the mind unfolds, the earliest being memory age, followed by the inquisitive age, which in turn is followed by the analytical age. This classification we make, ignoring the relations of sensation, perception, etc., which apply in secular education as they cannot in Sunday-school work.

I. Individual texts should be early memorized.

Great care should be taken in selecting those sentences that are to be made permanent dwellers in the mind. Those should be selected that adapt themselves to every man, to every human experience. They may be single verses or paragraphs, like the twenty-third Psalm, but they need to be practically independent of all other Scripture. They must point their own lesson, unfold their own truth without special knowledge of their associations when uttered. They must be rhythmical, that the thought and life shall vibrate harmoniously with the truth expressed. They must have the secret art of weaving themselves into the memory of the child, so that it shall be easier to retain the words once learned than to forget them.

The foundation of all systematic study of the Bible should be laid in a ready command, accurate and appreciative, of a large number of peculiarly effective texts. It is not enough to have these learned for a day, but they must be repeated until they are recalled unconsciously when needed.

A large part of the earliest years of Bible study should be devoted to memorizing texts and paragraphs. The power of verbal memory is at its height from six to twelve. This is not saying that it may not be cultivated to accomplish greater results later in life by a masterly use of the will, of laws of thought, etc.; but with the average — we may almost say the universal mind, the years of natural verbal memorizing are under twelve, or, at most, fourteen. With people whose after-life is not professional and scholastic, this is absolutely true.

The rule is that little Scripture will be accurately memorized and retained by those who do not acquire the relish and the habit under twelve or fourteen years of age. Children will memorize the rhythmical Scripture texts with delight as early as three years of age, if the texts are carefully selected. Before they are eight they may easily be taught almost indefinitely, provided they never have too much assigned, and care be taken in the selection.

The child mind is getting ready to study and think, and in this immature state it can feed profitably upon truths that are melodious, truths which stimulate its growth but make no effort to develop it. In the earliest years we have no moral right to develop the mind in the strict sense. We may feed it, we may direct its growth. It is difficult to state periods of change in years, but to those who will make due allowance for variation in children it may be safe to say that eight years is about as early as we can wisely do much by way of developing the powers of the mind. If we try to make them think, we attain no end, and merely destroy their relish for thought when the years come in which they should enjoy it.

The strawberry is the first fruit of the season. It is peculiarly delicious in taste. Its crisp, luscious freshness makes it a universal favorite. But it must be the first fruit to command its accustomed admiration. The late strawberry is doomed to disappointment. It finds the taste of the world otherwise occupied. So Scripture texts, the freshest, fairest, sweetest truth upon which the child mind can feed, if well chosen, in early years, are never the same in their relish afterwards. It is a matter of profound regret that the Revision Committee forgot the children when they took the verses out of the Bible, when they robbed it of its rhythm.

If the texts are learned, they will germinate their thought under proper leadership as soon as the mind has maturity to appreciate it. When the mind is prepared to think clearly, keenly, it is annoyed by the drudgery of memorizing. A person who sings by rote until he is sixteen will find it difficult to sing by note after that.

Very soon we may teach enough about the *truth* of the text to make it clearly appreciated. There are many advantages in having a text beautifully clothed. There is a disadvantage if we content ourselves with verbal memory. The rhythm results from a slightly figurative cast of the language. The very beauty of expression which makes it so easily remembered causes the meaning to escape unnoticed.

After verses are memorized, special attention should be given to making the meaning in its simplicity understood.

When there is a self-evident application to the truth, when it readily illustrates itself by a little direction, time and thought should be given to making the application. A truth is of little avail that is not applied, that is not at command and usable when needed. Every truth needs to be harnessed to real life, and the teacher must see to it that the child knows how to do it.

The life is to be fashioned by the truth learned in earliest years. In other words, the child is to learn how to adapt his life to the truth. By the age of ten or twelve it would seem reasonably easy to teach the important, standard, rhythmical verses, the truth they contain, illustrating and adapting them.

The mind in those years is getting its powers in readiness to think and reason. It is preparing itself and accumulating materials.

As the worm gives silk — the richest material for dress goods — to the world while he is getting ready to put forth his wings of beauty, so the mind, under proper training, may give to the entire character of a lifetime its richest vestments while it is getting ready to think and reason.

Ruskin tells us in one of his works that his knowledge of the Bible was largely confined to chapters that his mother had him memorize in boyhood. Upon these well-remembered passages of Scripture he has written and lectured much all these years. They are as follows: — Ex. 15, 20; 2 Sam. 1, from 7th verse; 1 Kings, 8; Ps. 23, 32, 90, 91, 103, 112, 119, 139; Prov. 2, 3, 8, 12; Is. 58; Matt. 5, 6, 7; Acts, 26; 1 Cor. 13, 15; James, 4; Rev. 5, 6.

' II. Teach the circumstances and associations of the truth as originally given. While many texts are clear without their setting, there are others that are literally meaningless until we know the customs of the times, the habits of the people. Teaching the geography or history as such is often ridiculed, but if these and other associative information are sought for the sake of making clear and vivid the truth of God, they are indispensable. In selecting texts to be memorized in early life, none should be chosen that need such explanation. The texts whose power is dependent upon an appreciative understanding of the time, manner, and circumstances of the utterance should come in gradually from eight to fifteen.

The associative aids of texts and truths are adapted to the inquisitive period of childhood, when the mind craves all possible explanatory and illustrative assistance. Special delight in biography, geography, and other incidentals of truth, begins gradually at about eight, and reaches its height at about fifteen, and then begins to wane. This period is nearly identical with the inquisitive years. The child under seven rarely asks questions inquisitively, except as they are suggested by some special need or striking circumstance. From twelve to fourteen the child will ask questions by the day, and that without anything, apparently, to suggest them. Much of the time he does not really care whether they are answered or not. He will skip from one thing to another with absolute revelry of delight in the mere privilege of asking questions. There are different degrees of this activity in different children, but the general fact abides that the inquisitive period begins gradually at about seven or eight, and ends at about fifteen.

During these years he should receive all the information possible. As we store his mind with texts in the early years, shading off our enthusiasm in them as he advances to the age of twelve, so we should begin to enlighten him regarding all the facts, incidents, customs, habits, etc., of the Bible at an average age of eight, and increase our attention to this matter up to fifteen.

The cyclamen, a rare little blossom, when it opens, rolls its petals back, curling them by the stem so as to bring the heart of the flower forward to the light. Thus the child, in the inquisitive years, seems chiefly desirous of having his mind get all the light upon truth that it can, and allows no pride or sensitiveness to prevent him from uncovering the truth to the light of every fact that be shed upon it. This is the time to teach everything that can aid the pupil to understand the Scripture.

III. Group the truths of the Bible with reference to human need. Group all the texts, incidents, historical facts, parables, etc., that bear upon the given subject. Without this systematic work we have not accomplished our mission. Above the age of fifteen, on the average, the mind makes new demands. It now seeks opportunities to use what it has acquired. The same spirit that gives uneasiness and the wish to leave school and get into business leads the youth to desire opportunity for original, independent, mental activity. He is no longer content with verbal memorizing, no longer desires to ask questions. The lad that at twelve asked questions indefinitely, even about things of which he did not care to know, will not, at eighteen, ask for information that he is really desirous of obtaining. He seems mortified that he does not know, and looks upon it as an exhibition of ignorance.

Teachers of young people from fourteen to twenty complain because they will not ask questions. It is not natural. It is not the inquisitive age. But, if properly handled, they will do more valuable work, will think for themselves with relish; but they must be started right. Their minds are naturally interested in classification, in analytical, logical considerations.

There is a tendency in youth to retire from the fireside, to be reticent with parents, and to drop out of Sunday-school. If their interest in home or church is to be retained, there must be a change in the method and manner. Even the affectionate, motherly way that was so caressingly tender and so warmly appreciated at twelve is sometimes repelled at seventeen. Parental authority has to be asserted judiciously or there is rebellion. Wise parents find ways by which to retain the affection, companionship, and control of their children through these years. Some teachers have an intuitive art by which they hold the interest and attention of the boys through these years, but more do not have the tact or secure the results. We must not be content until we retain most of the youth, and develop them into keen, devout, loyal students, and associates of Christian people.

There is no branch of study that will interest so many youth so thoroughly as the Bible, when it is analytically studied. Let pupils do their own searching, with such suggestions as the teacher may think wise to make. It will be slow work at first, but it pays in the familiarity it gives with the Bible, and the power attained to estimate the meaning of truth.

This practice will fix the texts in the mind more firmly, will give them new meaning, will impart intensity to their authority by emphasizing their utility.

This grouping may be made to take the place of doctrines, which are so loudly and indefinitely called for in some quarters. There are many biographical names about which texts may be grouped to advantage. Any name specially identified with the development of truth offers such advantages. For illustration, group the texts that relate to Abraham, throwing light upon his life and mission. Better than any amount of theory or abstract comment on the indorsement the New Testament gives the Old is the experience young people get in learning all they can of a patriarch like Abraham, finding references to him in Matthew, Mark, Luke, John, the Acts, Romans, Corinthians, Galatians, Hebrews, James, and Peter.

There is no better temperance lesson possible than to have the pupils search out for themselves all the texts that command sobriety, that emphasize the evils of drunkenness, that present a penalty for drunkenness, etc.

The Commandments gain immeasurably by the grouping about each such other Scripture as explains or emphasizes it. The Beatitudes in the same way gain greatly by grouping around each, texts that enlarge upon it.

For a general outline of grouping texts, historical incidents, parables, etc., there are advantages in taking them in this order, those relating to man, to Christ, to the Holy Spirit, to God.

Each of these would naturally be subdivided. It would follow the theological line better to reverse the order and group the texts that relate to God first, but our aim is to get results. The logic of results is to touch the pupil where his thought will count for most. The youthful mind will respond most readily to interests nearest at hand, most personal. The Word of God everywhere teaches of the Lord. Every text, coming as the authority of God, reveals somewhat his character. Beginning with God, our reasoning is inevitably abstract, and as the purpose of the Sunday-school is not to teach theology, but God's Word, we shall do that most effectively from the concrete side.

There are those who seem to have conscientious scruples against adapting even the thought or speech to youth, preferring to adapt youth to the standard of mature methods.

Fragrant flowers are always notional, and will never thrive except as the cultivation is adapted to them. Theoretically, plants need the sun, a warm climate, much moisture, and rich soil. Multitudes of plants will only grow away from the sun, others demand a cold climate, a dry soil, or sand. He who would raise plants on an abstract theory of the adaptability of sun, soil, climate, and heat, would find himself killing off most of the beauty he would possess.

It is a surprising fact that scarcely one fragrant plant meets the ideal requirements. Weeds are not notional; they always respond when abstract theories are applied. But weeds are never fragrant, — in the accepted sense. If we would develop youth in the love and power of the truth and its personal Author, we must adapt ourselves to the age, experiences, and necessities of those whom we would develop. The world is filled with weeds by means of the best endeavors ill-adapted to the end in view.

In illustrating the subdivision of subjects in grouping texts, the following is presented as a sample of a few divisions under MAN.

I. His Needs. — 1. Social: Relation to parents; relation to children; relation to friends; relation to enemies; relation to neighbors; business relations. 2. Personal: temporal; spiritual.

II. Consequences of Conduct. — 1. Of right doing; in present; in eternity. 2. Of wrong doing. 3. Of right speaking. 4. Of wrong speaking. 5. Of good companionship. 6. Of bad companionship.

To exemplify this more fully, a few Scripture references are given under Man's Social Needs: —

RELATION TO PARENTS.

Ye shall fear every man his mother and his father (Lev. 19: 3). Cursed be he that setteth light by his father or his mother (Deut. 27: 16). Hearken unto thy father that begat thee and thy mother when she is old (Prov. 23: 22). Honor thy father and thy mother, as the Lord thy God hath commanded thee: that thy days may be prolonged, and that it may go well with thee in the land which the Lord thy God giveth thee (Deut. 5: 16). What shall I do that I may inherit eternal life? . . . Honor thy father and thy mother (Luke 18 : 18, 19). Honor thy father and mother, which is the first commandment with promise, that it may be well with thee and thou mayest live long on the earth (Eph. 6: 23). My son, keep thy father's commandment, and forsake not the law of thy mother: bind them continually upon thine heart and tie them about thy neck (Prov. 6: 20, 21). Children, obey your parents in the Lord: for this is right (Eph. 6: 1). Children, obey your parents in all things: for this is well pleasing unto the Lord (Col. 3: 20). A wise son maketh a glad father: but a foolish son is the heaviness of his mother (Prov. 15: 20).

RELATION OF PARENTS TO CHILDREN.

And thou shalt teach them [the Scriptures] diligently to thy children (Deut. 6: 7, 8). Train up a child in the way he should go, and when he is old he will not depart from it (Prov. 22 : 6). Fathers, provoke not your children to anger, lest they be discouraged (Col. 3: 21.) Provoke not your children to wrath: but bring them up in the nurture and admonition of the Lord (Eph. 6: 4.) Correct thy son and he shall give thee rest; yea, he shall give delight unto thy soul (Prov. 29:17). The rod and reproof give wisdom; but a child left to himself bringeth his mother to shame (Prov. 29:15). Chasten thy son while there is hope (Prov. 13:18). He that spareth his rod hateth his son: but he that loveth him chasteneth him betimes (Prov. 13:24).

RELATION TO FRIENDS.

A man that hath friends must show himself friendly; and there is a friend that sticketh closer than a brother (Prov. 18:24). As in water face answereth to face, so the heart of man to man (Prov. 27:19). Can two walk together except they be agreed (Amos 3:3). A friend loveth at all times (Prov. 17:17). Faithful are the wounds of a friend (Prov. 27:6). Two are better than one . . . . for if they fall, the one will lift up his fellow: but woe to him that is alone when he falleth, for he hath not another to lift him up (Ec. 4:9, 10). Make no friendship with an angry man: and with a furious man thou shalt not go, lest thou learn his ways (Prov. 22:24, 25).

RELATION TO ENEMIES.

The soul of the wicked desireth evil: his neighbor findeth no favor in his eyes (Prov. 21:10). Love your enemies, bless them that curse you, do good to them that hate you, and pray for them that despitefully use you and persecute you (Matt. 5:44). And when ye stand praying, forgive, if ye have aught against any: that your Father also which is in heaven may forgive you your trespasses. But if ye do not forgive, neither will your Father which is in heaven forgive your trespasses (Mark 11:25, 26). Forgive us our debts, as we forgive our debtors (Matt. 6:12). Parable of the unmerciful servant (Matt. 18:23–35). Agree with thine adversary quickly, while thou art in the way with him (Matt. 5:25). If thou bring thy gift to the altar, and there rememberest that thy brother hath aught against thee; leave there thy gift before the altar, and go thy way; first be reconciled to thy brother, and then come and offer thy gift (Matt. 5:23, 24).

The more minute the subdivisions, provided there be texts to supply them, the closer the thought required in grouping and classifying truth, the greater the intellectual and moral benefit attained.

Beside such systematic research for texts with a view to a logical classification by their thought and application to specific need, how frivolous seems the exercise we sometimes witness of directing a school to search for the "hands," "eyes," "ears," "feet," etc., of the Bible.

The following are some of the minor benefits of this search for truths to meet specific needs: It renders independent thought both possible and profitable, and prompts to a right application of Scripture remedies to human necessities. It places teacher and pupils on a common footing, and brings them into sympathy by the development of a spirit of harmony in thought and interest. It leads to the formation of habits of applying Scripture, of looking at every passage to see where it fits into the affairs of every-day life.

The growing mind needs mental, Scriptural

food in abundance. The character of the mature mind depends upon it more largely than is generally supposed. A large man does not necessarily eat more than a small man. Size and food have no appreciable relation to each other in manhood. In youth, when size is being determined, the quantity of food usually represents growth. In mental, moral, and spiritual matters it is even more true that, as we feed and exercise the intellect, emotions, and will, we determine the maturity and power of the man.

Some phases of the development of the individual mind may be best learned by studying the development of mind in history. Take music as an illustration. For centuries there was no suspicion of any higher phase of music than Melody, or a succession of notes. It was not until the sixteenth century that there was any approach to Harmony, or the combination of simultaneous tones. It was not until the eighteenth century that, under Mozart and Haydn, the art of harmonizing instruments of different capacities was developed. In music, therefore, it was the appreciation of the simple, melodious notes of the scale that satisfied the ear and mind of the world for centuries. Then it was a knowledge of the simple relations of similar tones to each other; and when the taste and ear of the world were developed, there was a demand for the fullest and most complicated grouping of tones by every conceivable variety of instrument. Thus in the individual mind there is first an appreciation of the simple, beautiful texts of the Word of God; then there is an inquiry as to the relations of these truths to each other, and to the associations in which they were born; and lastly, there is a demand for every conceivable grouping of these truths to make the most perfect and intricate harmony for the benefit of man and the glory of God.

ART OF THINKING.

"Thought alone is eternal." — OWEN MEREDITH.

"Thought is deeper than all speech." — CRANCH.

"The power of thought — the magic of the mind." — BYRON.

"Thought by thought piled, till some great truth is loosened."
— SHELLEY.

"What think ye of Christ?" — MATT. 22 : 42.

"When I was a child I thought as a child." — 1 COR. 13 : 11.

"They are never alone that are accompanied with noble thoughts." — SIDNEY.

"The child's reasoning powers are, as it were, the wings with which he will eventually have to fly." — LANDON.

"Not that we are sufficient of ourselves to think anything as of ourselves, but our sufficiency is of God." — 2 COR. 3 : 5.

CHAPTER II.

ART OF THINKING.

WHO can estimate the distance between an indistinct and a distinct thought? Who can measure the difference between inaccurate and accurate thinking? What is the distinction in power between a vague and a clear idea?

There is philosophy in thought. There is art in thinking.

The business man learns to think distinctly, accurately, clearly, without studying any art, without adhering to any philosophy. The native elasticity of an active mind in a vigorous body, the facility of the mind in adapting its methods in emergencies, the tendency of the mind to evolve a power of thought through experiment, gives a business or professional man a power of thought, a skill in thinking, without definite training. Trusting to the survival of the fittest, they come to have an effective, if not a scholastic, art of thinking.

No accidental art of thought is reliable in dealing with the truth of God. The truth, as far as it relates to the plan of salvation and the precepts of morality, is so clear that a wayfaring man, though a fool, need not err. The ignorance of many black preachers in the South has been a revelation of the possibilities of preaching the truth so far as the plan of salvation is concerned, while having no conception of the meaning of the Scripture which they entirely misused, but from which they drew another truth in itself correct.

We heard the Rev. John Jasper, in Richmond, preach his famous sermon on "The sun do move," in which he abused half a hundred texts scientifically, making the Scriptures teach that the patriarchs, prophets, Psalmist, apostles, and Christ teach that the sun "do move;" that it was a sin against God to attempt to measure the distance of the heavenly bodies; that the earth was not round, but flat, and had four corners. All the time that he was scientifically abusing the Scriptures, he pointed several grand truths morally and spiritually, and one of the grandest efforts to which we have listened was his incidental description of the passage of the Red Sea, illustrating it by reference to the recent deliverance of his own race, with whom he had been in slavery forty years.

None or all of these things, however, relieve the church of the responsibility of doing all it can to make the thought of the pulpit and pew distinct, accurate, clear, and loyal. A distinguishing feature of the human mind is its possibility of development. Its various faculties increase in strength, in discriminating skill, in rapidity and reliability of action, in permanency of effect through systematic training. The more correct and scientific the method, the more prompt and complete is its development.

The mind has peculiar attachment for any line of thought in which it is developed. It views with reverential awe any philosophy through which it has been disciplined. It follows enthusiastically any master who has led it to victory.

Soldiers care little for the personal characteristics of an officer, provided he be a brilliant commander in drill, a heroic leader in battle. So the mind swears hearty allegiance to philosophies with which it has no natural affiliation, and to masters with whom it has nothing in common, simply because the mental faculties delight in being marshalled, in their philosophic evolutions, under expert generalship.

The mind is never so content as when it receives its highest, broadest development in Bible philosophy. It follows no leaders more ardently than devout, intelligent, fervent Christian scholars and philosophers. There is no other line of study in which such perfection and vigor of development of the mind in its entirety is possible. Much of the skepticism and baneful philosophy of anti-Christian thought is due to lack of method and constancy of application on the part of those who should have led in the wise development of the mind.

The outline of method may be concisely stated.

I. Appreciation of single, simple facts and truths. In secular education the important thing in reasoning is to be clear, accurate, distinct in our premises. Processes of reaching conclusions are of no value if we are not skilled in the art of perception and conception in regard to initial facts. The foundations are nowhere more vital than here. The expert instructor in any art detains the pupil upon a few rudiments until his patience is nearly exhausted. After that he advances him rapidly. In penmanship it is a few initial strokes and movements; in drawing, a few lines and combinations; in music, a few notes, — that absorb the time.

In thinking, the foundation of success lies in the keenest, clearest power to handle individual facts. We must know single facts personally, as it were. We must have power to dissociate the abstract idea suggested from the concrete thing which suggested it. We must know every single thought without reference to the manner of its dress. Those who know people by their clothes, or even by their features, have an immature mind, while those who know them by dissociating the characteristics from all attachments of dress or peculiarities of feature have the mind in training for better work. The first condition of clear thought is appreciation of every fact and truth so as to recognize it in its essence, under whatever conditions it presents itself. The steps in the cultivation of this art are these:—

1. Appreciation of that which is present, which interests by its presence, by its active associations.

2. Appreciation of that which is present, but interests because of its suggestion of memories or past associations.

3. Appreciation of that which is present, but interests because of its suggestions of possibilities through the imagination, inventive genius, or otherwise.

4. Appreciation of that which is absent, but is recalled to the mind by memory or imagination.

Each of these steps indicates an advance in mental development, and whoever finds his appreciation of single facts or truths — present and absent — trustworthy, has the foundation of good thinking.

Nowhere is this distinction more important than in Bible study. We can scarcely dwell too long upon the fundamentals of Christian thought and Divine truth.

Definitions are very rarely taught in Sunday-school, and yet they are worth a whole system of theology without them. A clear apprehension of the meaning of terms used in theology, a wide dissemination of definite thought in regard to words and phrases used in theologic argument, would make theology interesting and profitable, where now it is dull, repulsive, and harmful. The last two chapters of this work deal with definitions so far as they are useful in those subjects, partly by way of illustration of the possibilities in this direction. We need to devote a large part of the time and energy of the Sunday-school to teaching the texts and truths that are fundamental.

II. Discrimination between facts or truths to note their differences. As soon as we appreciate facts or truths, we instinctively note dissimilarities, and the power which it indicates should be promptly, vigorously developed. The man who has permanent employment and the best pay in mechanics has this skill. It indicates the expert in any department. The courts recognize this mastery of mind, and will receive testimony which the rules otherwise exclude, if it be given by an expert who has acquired a reputation as well as proficiency in detecting differences at sight, understanding their significance. There are steps in the development of this art.

1. Skill in discriminating between things both of which are present. It is the earliest, most natural way of applying or developing the art. We all discriminate in things in which we are interested, and think it strange that others do not. The lady of fashion is haunted for weeks by bad taste. A certain art club of Boston memorialized the city government, in a most elaborate and formal way, to protect people of artistic taste from the "hideous and ridiculous" monuments, fountains, etc., "architectural and sculptural monstrosities," which have been inflicted on the city. These very objects of such bitter denunciations had been supposed to be beautiful by those who had no skill in artistic discrimination. Every member of that horrified club has his weaknesses, in which his tastes or opinions would be as hideous, ridiculous monstrosities as these fountains.

The author knows a farmer who was born and bred on a farm, and has handled cattle from early boyhood, and at the age of fifty is bothered to tell which is the "nigh ox" of the yoke. But that man knows every butterfly, bug, or other insect at sight that ever flew in that county.

2. Skill in discriminating between facts, thoughts, truths, one of which is absent. The physician's success in the diagnosis of a case lies in his power to distinguish between the symptoms of the case in hand and one that is not present. Frequently he is discriminating between an actual present case and an ideal case that in its details never occurred.

The lawyer requires a similar power to imagine or recall a case, and then make the jury discriminate between this case and that.

This phase of Bible study has been too long ignored. Every truth, after it is distinctly known, needs to be discriminated from other truth. One of the remarkable things about the Word of God is the fact that, while it is so plain that the "wayfaring man" need not misunderstand any moral or spiritual truth it teaches, at the same time its fullest meaning necessitates the most delicate exactness in so small a matter as emphasis and inflection. Although the same truth seems told several times, it is questionable whether there is an instance in which, taking the associations into account, there is any truth stated in two places in the Bible in which there is not a shade of difference. Even the same text written in Matthew and Luke has a slightly different force because of the different intent of the chronicler, and the different attitude of the audience.

The incident recorded in John 4: 9–26 — the woman of Samaria — gets much of its force from the discriminating emphasis of verse 18, "Thou hast well said, I *have* no husband; for thou hast had *five* husbands: and *he* whom thou *now* hast is not thy *husband;* in that saidst thou truly." This shows by emphasis what otherwise might not appear, that she was living a disreputable life.

In John, chapter 21, occur the words, "Lovest thou me?" in three successive verses. Clear discrimination gives peculiar force to each question, which would be entirely lost if there were but one, and is lost if they are all read in the same way. " Lovest *thou* me more than these?" " Lovest thou *me?*" " *Lovest* thou me?" Even the original is different in the last case to emphasize the peculiarly tender, personal and emphatic love that is intended as in distinction from the other queries.

There is strong temptation to continue these illustrations, but from those already given it will be readily seen how much scope there is for unfolding a Bible within the Bible, — a new text in almost every text in the Scriptures. The teacher gains power to make the Word of God the most fascinating of studies when she trains her pupils to love to discriminate sharply, to seek what the text does not mean, and what it does mean, that no other Scripture does.

III. Skill in comparing facts, thoughts, truths, with a view to noting resemblances. This is a constructive art, and is of a higher grade than the last. Critics are usually men who have developed the art of noting differences without the positive virtue of observing resemblances. Morose, caustic, uncomfortable people are usually those who have trained themselves to observe the dissimilarity in men, in circumstances, in truth, while the genial, hopeful, joyous members of society are those who have accustomed themselves to look for resemblances.

This art must be built upon the former. Those who see only the hopeful side of affairs are as unsafe as the other extreme is uncomfortable. The high art is in knowing how to analyze and discriminate sharply, and then out of the differences build up from resemblances. Theology that shall command the respect of all classes of thoughtful minds, irrespective of inherited prejudices, will be the grouping of similar truths, after they have been sharply discriminated, having been first clearly appreciated. There are few tributes to divine wisdom more direct, simple, and grand than that which the Bible pays to man's possibilities through the triune deity, when, without any theological attempt, we appreciate truth, discriminate in the study of it, and then classify it according to its resemblances. It is like the chemist's art in placing a substance in solution, keeping it thus until it has lost its crude affinities, allowing it then to crystallize according to the higher laws of its nature.

Theology is only allowable when it is the crystallized beauty and glory of the truth as it is in the Word of God.

IV. Skill in estimating the consequences of facts, thoughts, and truths neglected, rejected, or applied. Thought is not mature until it is materialized. A theory that will not work in practice; an invention that cannot be made to do what, in the abstract, it can be made to appear to do; a profession that is not possession in character, — is useless.

There are numberless men who have made a hundred fortunes in the abstract, who never paid their honest bills a single month of their life. The shores of financial life are strewn with men who were rich so long as they could pass their credit for goods, but were disgraced as soon as the creditors tried to realize. The Patent Office is the receptacle of hundreds of thousands of inventions, most of which lacked the practical element of estimating the consequences of an application of their principle. There are multitudes of men of eminent learning, of extraordinary power of thought, theoretically, who are comparatively worthless members of society because they cannot apply their thought. They can link their chariot to a star, but not to earth.

A physician of comparatively slight professional training, provided he have thorough training in the fundamentals, may succeed where the most learned fail, by acquiring practical skill in estimating promptly and discriminatingly the effect of treatment. In the legal profession the same truth is verified by experience. In the ministry, in teaching, in literature, it is the same. The scholarly men for whom the world has no need console themselves with the fact that the world likes to be humbugged, and only humbugs succeed, but the fact remains that with insignificant exceptions the world wants men of brains, but of brains applied to real life.

The spider eats double quantity, — part for its life, and part for the purpose of spinning webs. When it ceases to spin, it ceases to eat, and dies eventually because it will not spin. Men with brains must feed their minds doubly well, for the sake of growth and of development, or the use of its knowledge and power for the world's enlightenment. Men who will not weave their thoughts into the network of daily life must be content with the mental dyspepsia which leads to uselessness and unhappiness.

The virtue of the Bible is in the application

of its truth. It was written, as no other book ever was, to be applied. It has no merit until it is rooted in action. Oats placed on cotton in a glass of water will sprout promptly and grow with fabulous rapidity for a few days, but will never stalk up or bear grain. They must be rooted in the earth if they are ever to become food in stalk or seed.

Truth can only benefit the possessor or the world when it is rooted in every-day life.

The power of teaching the Word of God is measurable by the thought developed, and the application made in the disposition, in the acts towards friends and enemies, in habits of speech, in worship, and in spirituality.

The story is told of a man who quoted the Bible fluently; who had an unctuous tone; who went everywhere but to his own church'; who found attendance upon public meetings, conventions, etc., a luxury that he could not deny himself; who never heard sermons, preferring to go where he could talk. His business was neglected, his home unprovided for, and his poor, broken-down, overworked wife had all the care of a large family without proper means of support. A lady who had heard the husband at a public gathering called upon the half-sick wife to tell her how much good her dear husband was doing, and was quite confounded with the truthful comment of the wife, that her husband *always lived his religion away from home.* Such professed Christians dishonor the truth.

There is a false and a true way of teaching the application. There are those — and they are not few, nor are they confined to the unlettered — who use the Word of God to illustrate their own thought. It is astonishing how many there are of this class, who, with voice and pen, put their thought first, make their own application of their thought, and then pick up some text to illustrate it. Without assuming to criticise such a method, — for it is the purpose of these pages to avoid direct criticism, — we cannot forbear calling attention to the fact that the art of correct and vigorous thinking would seem to demand that we seek to appreciate the truth as God has given it, irrespective of its influence upon us. We need to discriminate sharply the special significance of the text to know why it was given as it was. We need to compare the various important truths, grouping them for their combined power, and, knowing what the truth is, apply it in our lives and make them conform thereto.

We may well distrust any leader who uses the Bible to indorse any philosophy or justify any action. It is safe to confide in him who seeks to harmonize his thought and life with the truth of God.

The art of correct thinking, then, demands that we think vigorously, keenly, promptly enough to sway the words and acts of our life into harmony with God's Word.

V. Reasoning inductively. We form many judgments without any appreciable process. If we have done the initial work with sufficient care and thoroughness, the conclusions will be safe and reliable. The habit of doing the early work correctly will project itself into the reasoning process and make that passable. Appreciation of single truths; discrimination of differences; comparison of resemblances; estimate of consequences, prompt us to form right judgments without any formality of processes. We are confident in our judgments; but if we are logically or sophistically assailed, we have no good and sufficient reason to give for our loyalty to our judgments. There is no liability of our judgment being wrong, even if we have no knowledge of or skill in logic. In preparation for assaults on our own faith, at least, we need to be equipped with the fundamentals of logic.

Inductive reasoning is the process by which we draw a concise conclusion from many facts, observations, or experiences. We begin with the effects and discover or conclude the cause. A definition is the result of inductive reasoning. We group the characteristics of anything into a definition. We append several examples of this process.

1. The bean grows, so does the cabbage and the cauliflower. These are vegetables. We know of no vegetable that does not grow. We reach the conclusion, therefore, by induction, that all vegetables grow.

2. The tansy grows, so does the motherwort. These are herbs, and as we know of no herbs that do not grow, we reach the conclusion inductively that all herbs grow.

3. The currant-bush and rose-bush grow, they are shrubs. We proceed until we conclude that all shrubs grow.

4. We may conclude from the apple-tree, maple, oak, and pine that all trees grow.

5. Vegetables, herbs, shrubs, and trees are plants. These all grow. We know of no plants that do not grow. We conclude, therefore, that all plants grow.

Whether we appreciate it or not, a large part of our judgments are formed by this process.

The principle upon which inductive reasoning rests is simply that what is true of every constituent part is true of the constituted whole. It is chiefly important that we be correct and careful in our observations of the particulars: that we consider the various individuals from the same standpoint or in regard to the same quality or phase: that we generalize comprehensively and with care: that we state our conclusions accurately and clearly.

VI. Deductive reasoning. This is the art by which we start from a general truth, and one special truth that may be connected with it, and deduce a third new truth. What we have just said in introducing inductive reasoning is equally pertinent here. Many form correct judgments, if previously well trained in the fundamentals of thought, without any appreciated logical process, and they are content with their positions, and with reason, so long as they are left alone. No one is equipped for intelligent self-defence, however, until he understands the principles of deductive reasoning.

It is an art applied by the sophist with so much trickery that, even when fairly well equipped for logical combat, it is judicious to be not over-anxious to face a foe.

All logic rests upon three principles so simple that no one questions their reliability, and upon the universality of their acceptance rests the authority of logic.

1. Whatever is, is.
2. Nothing can both be and not be at the same time.
3. Everything must either be or not be.

It may not seem important to give special thought to truths so simple as these, but the security of the superstructure depends upon the foundation, and we can hardly be too careful to understand all that is involved in these three statements, and they should be at our command as the multiplication table is. These principles are stated in logic as laws:—

1. The Law of Identity. *Whatever is, is.*
2. The Law of Contradiction. *Nothing can both be and not be at the same time.*
3. The Law of Excluded Middle. *Everything must either be or not be.*

Of the first law nothing need be said. Of the second, we may caution students to apply it sharply. We are liable to be wrecked by the application of it if we do not take time and give thought sufficient to be sure that we take in an object or thought in its entirety. It is one of the tricks of sophistry to show a part of a thing, prove that a special thing is true of it, and then demand, on the ground of the second law, that we conclude that to be true of the whole. The story of the shield is familiar. Each seeing but one side affirmed that what was true of what he saw was true of the whole. We can only apply this principle with confidence of that portion of a thing which we see or know. If one appreciate single, simple truths; if he have skill in discriminating, skill in comparing, skill in application, he is safer without logic than logic is without training in the fundamentals.

Nowhere is this second law more generally abused than in consideration of God and his dealing with men. Not a few good men, intelligent men, are afraid of logic because it has been and is so cruelly abused. This is an argument for knowing more of it and not less. A little logic may be a dangerous thing, but not if that little is confined to the fundamentals, and whatever is known is well known. It is the trick of sophists to view some special phase of the Lord's dealing with men, and then, in the name of this second law, demand that that shall be accepted as the character of God. There is no place where logic is so unsatisfactory as in application to Divine things, because of the improbability of our getting an entire view of the phase of character or relations of parties involved in the consideration. It is not needed, as already remarked, in forming personal judgments, so much as in guarding against the assaults of others. We question the propriety of taking the initiative in appealing to logic, but believe that no Christian is so safe, intellectually at least, without thorough fortification in the principles of logic as with them. The second law is the one most liable to be abused in the consideration of Divine truth.

The third law seems more vague and non-essential than the others, and yet its importance cannot be over-estimated. It rests upon the principle that everything must either be or not be. In other words, it simply insists that every proposition be so stated that it can be answered by *yes* or *no*, and then insists that it be so answered. It states that a thing *is* or *is not*. Most of the loose thought of the world as well as loose morality grows out of not insisting upon this requirement. So long as we ignore it and leave our propositions where they can be equivocally answered, or accept such answers to more definite propositions, there is no security to logic; and if the same permission be granted in action, then there is no security to character. The Scripture saith wisely when it saith (Matt. 5 : 37), "Let your communication be, Yea, yea; Nay, nay:

for whatsoever is more than these cometh of evil."

This third law demands that everything be so definitely and clearly stated that there shall be no hesitancy or reservation in saying "Yes" or "No" to the proposition. It must be easy to accept or reject promptly the statement or truth involved. It is worth more than may appear upon the surface to know our rights in this regard, and nowhere is it so valuable as in Bible study with those who incline to put us on the defensive.

After consideration of the chapter on Belief, it will be more readily seen that the Christian who intelligently believes the truth of God, and has had it sealed by a personal experience, needs never appeal to logic, but may find it serviceable to understand it when others use it to dethrone faith. Our attitude is such that it is the part of wisdom to insist that, if our antagonists incline to argue, they shall be made to frame their own propositions. Since there is, in the nature of the case, almost no possibility of winning a soul to the truth by argument, we have little occasion to appeal to it for that purpose.

The difficulty at once presents itself that there are many questions or propositions that cannot be answered by Yes or No. Logically, there is no difficulty in this, for there is no proceeding except as we say unequivocally that a thing is or that it is not. Mathematically there is a third position, but not logically. In mathematics there may be the question of quantity or degree, but not in logic.

We cannot say logically that one thing is harder or softer, warmer or colder, than another. We may say it is hard or that it is not hard; that it is soft, or that it is not soft. If we say that it is not hard, and that it is not soft, we give a pretty distinct idea of its relative position in the scale of hardness.

In logic it is not equivalent to saying that anything has the reverse if we say that it has not a specific quality. We have no right to infer what is true from an announcement of what is not true. If I say that truth is not triangular, I do not imply that it has any other geometrical form.

The secret of the necessity of employing Deductive Reasoning lies in the fact that there is a field untouched and unreachable by direct appreciation of truth, by the discrimination of truths, by the comparison of truths. It applies to truths that in the nature of the case cannot be compared directly, but must be compared, if at all, with some third standard with which each can in turn be compared. I want to know which of two rooms is the larger. I cannot bring the two together, but I can compare the dimensions of each with a yardstick, and with that as a third or middle term I can compare the rooms with each other. This is not the manner in which comparisons are made logically, and yet illustrates in a certain sense why it is essential and how it may be done.

There are three logical axioms that need to be given in connection with the principles already announced. In each statement of the logical process there are two premises, the chief and the less, — or, technically, the major and the minor, — and the conclusion. The axioms are these, —

1. Two terms agreeing with one and the same third term agree with each other.

Major. Fixed stars are self-luminous.

Minor.   Sirius is a fixed star.
Conclusion.   Therefore Sirius is self-luminous.

2. Two terms, of which one agrees and the other does not agree with one and the same third term, do not agree with each other.

Major.   Planets are not self-luminous.
Minor.   Venus is a planet.
Conclusion.   Venus is not self-luminous.

3. Two terms, both disagreeing with one and the same third term, may or may not agree with each other.

Major.   Planets are not self-luminous.
Minor.   Sirius is not a planet.

Both these are true, but no conclusion is possible. The fact is, that Sirius is self-luminous, but there is nothing in these two premises to show that it is.

It is needless to say that we make no attempt to teach logic. We have given thus much, because it has seemed to be made necessary by what went before. We repeat what we have more than once said already, that it is infinitely more important to be skilful in the first four steps here laid down than in either Inductive or Deductive Reasoning.

Under eight or nine years of age the child merely appreciates single, simple truths. From eight to fifteen he acquires skill in discriminating and comparing things, thoughts, truths. Prior to fifteen or sixteen he is merely collecting material for thought, and is exercising his faculties for use when he is matured. If we feed his mind from the Bible, if we give it systematic exercise in learning, appreciating, discriminating, comparing its truths and estimating the consequences, we are morally certain that his mature thought and logic will be loyal to the truth as it is in the Word of God.

ATTENTION.

"My son, attend to my words." — PROV. 4 : 20.

"Attend to know understanding." — PROV. 4 : 1.

"Attend to the words of my mouth." — PROV. 7 : 24.

"Attention narrows our mental working into one channel."
— LANDON.

"Attention is the co-ordinating and controlling force exerted by the mind upon its various powers, so as to bring into strongest action this or that particular phase of its activity." — LANDON.

"Clear and vivid conception implies attention. To establish the power of attention is at first a trying effort both for pupil and teacher. Without this, even natural acuteness will accomplish little."
— CURRIE.

"Attention is necessary to the correct use of all the faculties. . . . It affects all sides of the intellect, and is one of the very foundations upon which memory is built." — LANDON.

CHAPTER III.

ATTENTION.

THE object of mental discipline is to know where to place the attention to greatest profit, how to get it there quickest, and keep it there most intently. Intellect, emotion, and will are all at their best when the mind gives attention most profitably. None need this power more than those who would know the truth of God as it is in his Word.

Every teacher appreciates the difficulty of gaining and retaining the attention of a class. There is an inborn art by which some teachers hold the eye and ear, the thought and affection of the pupils. There are laws by which the non-magnetic teacher is aided in securing, in fair degree, what the more favored teacher gains by natural tact. The former would intensify power, while the latter would conserve force and make it permanent by appreciating the philosophy of attention.

When anything unusual attracts the ear or eye, we give heed to it without an act of the will. Indeed, it requires a strong act of the will not to give attention. This is styled involuntary attention. If we continue our observation after the surprise is over, because we desire to know more about it, that requires an act of the will, and is styled voluntary attention.

A child's earliest attention is involuntary, while that which comes from the experience of necessity, or results from instruction, is voluntary. It is useless to ask attention of young children. You must not demand, but win it, not by artfulness, but by art. The first aim is to win involuntary attention, and through patience by imperceptible transitions, train the scholars to *will* continued attention.

In acquiring the art of attention we must clearly classify the various phases in which it may be exercised.

No one can, in the nature of the case, acquire this art to a high degree in every line. Paradoxical as it may seem, the art of attention is non-attention. The greater our power of not attending to nine things may be our power in considering effectively the tenth. One of the first steps in learning how to attend is to learn how not to. The humming-bird never flies towards its nest, but, when it proposes to go there, it shoots up into the air and then drops into it almost imperceptibly. So, when the mind proposes to attend to anything, it seems to desert everything, and drops upon that one line of thought or investigation with peculiar tenacity.

Attention may be external or internal, may devote itself to that to which the senses attach it, or to abstract considerations. Both are important acquisitions of power, and must be cultivated, but at different times and by different art.

Skill in attending through the senses to what transpires about us must be acquired in early life. There is nothing, perhaps, in the whole range of mental training more important than accuracy in observing what passes about us. Clearness of perception and conception depend largely upon the art of being attentive to objects and events.

The first requisite is attention to those things

in which we are interested through the senses, but we must not stop there. Many are content with so much of attentive power as this. Animals have this. The beaver can build a dam, adapting the strength of every part to the current of water at that point. Even the lower animals attend to whatever they are interested in through their senses.

The second step to which the child must be advanced is that of attention through the senses to that in which he should be interested, regardless of whether he is or not. The moment we lift ourselves to the plane where we are indifferent to the tendencies of the senses in their likes and dislikes, and consider simply whether or not we need to attend to any object or event, we have taken a long stride intellectually.

The eagle perched on a dead branch away from the refreshment of shade, or musical rustle of foliage, with his eye scanning every object in the horizon, equally indifferent to all attractions until he sees the kingfisher dart into the water for prey, and then gives his sole attention to that bird as he emerges with a fish upon which the eagle proposes to feed, is an example in one direction of the skill that should be attained of being indifferent to all sense-attractions that are not profitable, putting all energy into those that promise us good.

Sir William Hamilton says the *intensity* of attention is in inverse ratio to its *extensity*. It is only as we train ourselves what not to notice that our observation of anything is valuable.

The third step is the attainment of power to attend to abstract thoughts unaided by objects, independent of senses. Children who always add by counting their fingers illustrate a large class of people who never find it easy to do any thinking without directly or indirectly leaning their thought upon something tangible.

Applied to Bible study, these steps mean : —

Learning texts because of their rhythm and verbal fascination.

Learning texts because we need the truth they contain.

Grouping texts according to their truth for the sake of higher phases of truth radiated by the blending of many truths.

In proportion as we have the power to attend, do we have control of circumstances instead of being controlled by them. Without this power in its external and internal phases one is the slave of events, the servant of men of stronger wills. Men influence us who have no business to do it, simply because we have neglected to train ourselves to *attend* to our own affairs.

The humming-bird sails up to a delicate flower on whose petals a tempting insect is feeding, and then "hums" his wings until he practically mesmerizes the little bug that forgets to attend to its own safety until he furnishes a delicate morsel for the bird. Thus those who have neglected the art of attention, whose teachers have neglected it, fall a prey to skeptical, seductive men. We benefit our pupils physically, morally, and religiously, as well as mentally, when we impart the power of giving intense, well-directed attention.

In class work we must appeal to the eye and ear by something new and distinct, bright and vivid, rhythmical and melodious. The familiar must be set in unfamiliar surroundings, or introduced at an unexpected time. We may find aid also, if we exercise wise caution by suggesting pleasure or pain, creating fear, or exciting hope.

The teacher will be aided in the accomplishment of this by asking questions with animation, as though the thought were new; by looking into the eye of the child, communicating thought by the look. This art of looking into the face of a child benignantly is attainable by most teachers, and has a magnetic influence in winning involuntary attention.

The questions asked and the thought imparted need to be vivid and suggestive. Illustrations should be bright, attractive, and familiar. The language should have the characteristics of everyday life; the voice should be mellow, animated, and winning.

That which requires especial caution in its use is the suggestion of pleasure or pain, fear or hope, raising expectation of reward for obedience, or punishment for disobedience. Much harm may be done by injudicious appeals through these channels.

There is attention that is fruitless of good. That which is desired is attention to the teacher for the sake of the lesson, in order to attract to the truth, and to God as the source of all truth. The teacher is to use devices, is to let himself down to the scholars, only that he may gain their attention, and fix it upon the lesson. They will seize upon and appropriate any truth that is made sufficiently simple and interesting.

If the class masters the teacher and holds him down to their level, the lesson is a failure. He must have the nerve and elasticity to lift them above their level, above himself even, to the great truths of the lesson.

The teacher must take the involuntary attention when won, and through it impart that desire for knowledge which shall make the pupil *will* attention. Ultimate success lies in teaching to desire to know the truth and impart such a habit of *willing* it that they attend without effort, giving voluntary attention involuntarily or unconsciously. So long as an effort is required to give attention, the attention itself cannot be most effective.

The adaptation of this phase of the teacher's work to the age of the pupils is of vital importance. No one, perhaps, ever tried harder to win the attention and love of children than Samuel Taylor Coleridge, who would watch for the children going from school to tell them stories, but he repulsed them all, and they styled him "Old Coley," shunning him in every way they could. He simply shot over their heads. He could not adapt himself to them, and there was a reason for this. He was one of the men of whom we have too many now, whose thought is on the correctness and finish of what they say, rather than on the capabilities and necessities of those whom they address. Charles Lamb told a good story of Coleridge, which, even if we do not demand that it be literally true, illustrates this characteristic of Coleridge. He met Lamb one day, and, seizing him by the button, began pouring forth a stream of philosophy in which Lamb had no conceivable interest. So he slyly took out his knife, cut the button off, and spirited himself away, all unknown to Coleridge, who held the button and talked on, and Lamb returned long afterward to find him still pouring forth his stream of philosophy. Extravagant as it is, it illustrates a tendency of many who fail to gain and retain attention from lack of adaptability to their hearers, especially to the age of those taught.

The adaptation of this phase of the teacher's work to the age of the pupils is of vital importance. Until the child has the maturity of the average child of seven or eight years, little or no effort should be made to win attention to abstract truths. In secular schools we say they should be taught objectively till then. In the Sunday-school they should have those texts whose meaning is clear and attractive, whose language is rhythmical, and whose application appears without much explanation or effort of thought. Melody of sound and attractiveness of truth must be to the Sunday-school what the object lesson is to the day-school.

From eight to fifteen there is to be gradual divorce from the application of art in winning attention through the senses. The teaching must shade off from sense appeals as fast as the mind is prepared for it. At fifteen, ordinarily, dependence upon sense interest in giving attention to a subject should cease. If the pupil has been well trained, he will be independent of all arts to hold the attention, having acquired the power to keep the mind to its work.

Through the telescope we see stars by day as

well as by night. It is only the unaided eye that has its attention so diverted by the brilliantly diffused sunlight as to lose sight of the beauties of the heavens. There is no subject upon which it is so hard to fix the attention under ordinary training as upon the truth of God. "The cares of this world, and the deceitfulness of riches, and the lusts of other things entering in," divert the attention, so that it is difficult oft-times for untrained minds to follow the prayer of another, the reading of the Scripture, or even a sermon.

The mind must be educated to command the thought through the will, as the telescope commands the eye, through its medium, to look at stars in broad day. Until the teacher has assisted the pupils to the attainment of this power, the work committed to him is not done.

When this skill is acquired, the scholar may, with comparative ease, be trained to such habits of voluntary attention that he shall think along the line of his work involuntarily, and, so far as any effort of the will is concerned, unconsciously. There is a waste of mental energy so long as will power is required to attend to any labor or truth; and it is equivalent to the creation of mental force to liberate the stimulus used in keeping the attention to any effort.

All praise to the leaders of the Primary Departments who have introduced song, blackboard, chart, picture, and concert exercises. But let it never be lost sight of that all the purpose these serve is to win the attention of young children whose minds have not developed the power of will indispensable to voluntary attention. These devices are not for show, but for a purpose. When used as an entertainment, when the child is permitted to depend upon them, when they take the place of memorizing Scriptures, these things become a hindrance. Their one work is to attract the attention until the teacher can secure their continued thought without such aids.

We must recognize, also, the mental transformation which culminates from fifteen to eighteen. The child must be brought into a state of independence of all arts in holding the thought to its work. He must thereafter be taught to give attention to his work on principle, forming habits of attention from interest and purpose without any effort of the will.

There is another practical use to which the art or possibilities of attention should be put, viz., to sight-reading of the Bible. It is a humiliating fact that no book is read with so little heed as the Word of God. There are times with most people when, if, after reading a chapter in this sacred volume, they should be asked to tell of what they have been reading, they could give but the merest outline, if even that. There is no excuse for this, since no book is so easily read attentively as the Bible. The only difficulty is that no attempt has been made to provide for this.

Marvellous results have been attained by those who have sought to develop skill in seeing the greatest number of things at sight in a given window. Almost anyone can, in a short time, acquire the ability to attend so keenly that he can pass a store-window at ordinary speed and see more than a score of things at sight, and remember them. We can attain the skill to pass through a library and at sight observe and remember as many volumes, telling the name, author, and color of each book.

A little judicious training in Scripture sight-reading will give power to read any chapter reasonably simple and interesting, and give all the details of its teaching. Select at first only a few verses; those that are clear and fascinating. The historic incidents in the Old Testament are good. Spend five minutes at the opening of each session in having the scholars read some short selection to themselves; then, closing the Bible, ask one or more to recite all that is remembered.

Such an exercise takes the thought from all other outside things: fixes it on the Bible; quickens their thought; awakens the attention. You will gain more time than the exercise has taken. An occasional exercise of this kind, at least, would be profitable.

THE ART OF REMEMBERING.

"Memory, the warder of the brain." — SHAKESPEARE.

"Hail, memory, hail! in thy exhaustless mine
From age to age unnumbered treasures shine!"
— ROGERS.

"Recollection is the only paradise from which we cannot be turned out." — RICHTER.

"Remember now thy Creator in the days of thy youth."
— ECCL. 12 : 1.

"Memory is the treasure-house of the mind." — FULLER.

"Persons who possess the power of keeping a large number of consciously-stored ideas just ready for use, and who can at once bring them forward when wanted, are said to be possessed of a good memory." — LANDON.

"If I do not remember thee, let my tongue cleave to the roof of my mouth." — Ps. 137 : 6.

CHAPTER IV.

THE ART OF REMEMBERING.

THE Bible needs to be so taught that its truths, the words in which they are clothed, the circumstances attending their utterance, and their application to man's need, shall be retained by the mind. In Bible teaching, little or no appeal can be made to the senses; hence the necessity of some method which shall give a correct knowledge of the Word of God, ability to retain it, and facility in recalling it so that it may be available when needed.

A truth to be remembered needs to be definitely, accurately, firmly fixed in the mind, with closely-affiliated associations, such that, when any one of these facts or incidents is remembered, it shall inevitably recall the truth itself. We do not remember that which is indefinite when we learn it, because it is blurred like the photograph of a child that moves before the camera.

When texts become familiar, while the truth they teach is indefinite, they will not be recalled when needed. Accuracy is equally important, since much of the looseness in theologic thought, much of the tendency to question the reliability of Scripture, results from lack of accurate knowledge of the phraseology of texts, of the exact meaning and special significance of words.

A fact or truth must be firmly fixed. Time must be taken, or special skill exercised, to assimilate or weave it into the mind, or it will never reappear. Many things that we think we learn soon fade, like the proof of the photographer upon exposure to the sun.

Memory, like a panorama, passes events in review, grouping them into families or landscapes, refusing to give place to any dissociated fact, homeless waif of thought, or uncompanionable idea. Our knowledge of Biblical truth, therefore, needs to be affiliated as closely as possible with everything of interest that will fraternize with it.

The attitude of the mind toward truth when it is learned determines largely the power of retaining the thought then matured. Our interest in a truth, other things being equal, measures its grip upon our mind, because we see most readily and vividly that which we like best, and it abides with us a proportionately long time. Those matter-of-fact critics who think it all sentiment when we emphasize the necessity of pupils loving the teacher, the school, and the lesson, must be ignorant of the fact that no philosophy is better established than that love for a truth learned, and for all the associations in which it is learned, is essential to its secure attachment to the mind. Hence arises the responsibility of parents and others in weaving about the child a network of pleasant associations in connection with whatever pertains to the church and Sunday-school, their officers and members. Every criticism is an attack upon the child's interest in, or love for the truth of God, and by interposing an unpleasant association is liable to rob the child of truth in which his eternal interests are involved.

Forgetfulness is such a recognized bane in human experience that the teacher is inexcusable if he does not use every means at his command to enlighten his pupils in the art of not forgetting what has been once known.

Bible truth is liable to be so disconnected with other knowledge and daily life as to become a companion piece to "Sunday religion," and never be recalled except at church or prayer meeting. It requires wise and patient teaching to so establish truth that it shall be remembered at all times when it can be of service.

Recalling past knowledge is a phase of the art of remembering that needs to receive special attention. It is sometimes an involuntary, sometimes a voluntary, mental act. Whenever the mind is not employed in active effort, it usually entertains itself with a panorama of what it has previously known. Such is the native elasticity of the mind, and so great is its enjoyment of its own treasures, that it recounts its wealth of memories. Its resources are so inlinked with each other down to the active present that, when at our best, we can scarcely see, hear, or learn anything without involuntarily recalling a chain of instances in our past experiences.

For illustration, I meet a lady in the horsecars, who, though a stranger, has a hand-satchel that reminds me of the only other one I ever saw like it, that was carried by another stranger on a Western train ten years ago. That recalls the excursion I was then taking, and I run over a series of incidents until I am once more in San Francisco. I recall attending church, recall the text, the peculiar way it was handled, the good impression it made. This leads me to recall the preacher, and I pass in review the various ways in which I have known of him, and it occurs to me that I heard that he desires a change of pastorate, and I interest myself in him, and he secures such a field as he desires.

The entire line of recollection was involuntary. One incident followed another because, when it occurred, it was linked to the one next to it. We may voluntarily recall an event by the same process; in which case, knowing what we wish to recall, we bring to mind everything in our past experience that would be liable to be associated with the person, place, name, etc., we aim to recall. With skill and patience we may voluntarily recall almost anything we have ever known.

The science of not forgetting anything is to associate it with things most likely to suggest it in time of need. Whoever trains himself to dovetail his knowledge into the activities of life is almost certain to have it recall itself when needed; and if it does not, it reduces to the minimum the labor of recalling it by the exercise of the will.

The success of Sunday-school teaching lies largely in having every truth so related to human need, to other truth, and to the Author of all Truth, that whenever any experience needs a Divine truth, it involuntarily recalls it through the law of association, or makes it an easy matter to recall it voluntarily. The way truth is learned determines the tenacity with which it is remembered and the facility with which it is recalled.

While it is possible for a truth to be so vividly impressed at first as to be permanently retained and readily available, it is so rare an experience as to be considered an improbable occurrence. A single impression seldom suffices for permanency. It is, as a rule, only a question of time for the erasure of the impression of a truth considered but once. If, after it has been thus obliterated, it be reconsidered, it is, to all intents and purposes, the meeting of a new truth. The keener the attention when a truth is learned, the less need of repetition. It is a time-saving process, therefore, to acquire such skill in attention as to reduce the waste of time in reconsideration to the minimum.

Into everything that is well learned we spin a part of our best self, our thought. Our knowledge, when it is acquired with interest, is like the web of the spider, who puts himself into it, and still retains such a sensitive connection with it that to touch any thread touches the insect himself. Our knowledge should be such that to touch it at any point is to make everything connected with it alive in memory.

Every truth needs to be reviewed and its expression repeated so frequently as to make it practically inerasable. Each truth should be reconsidered until its echo becomes perpetual in the mind. Frequent repetition of a truth is a substitute for strenuous mental effort in attention. There is no virtue in repetition except as it gets a firmer grip of thought each time.

The melody of Bible language cannot be over-estimated as an aid in remembering and recalling the truth which the texts enshrine. Words symbolize ideas, and well chosen words convey ideas that become loyal residents of the mind. The teacher, therefore, who holds the text before his scholars in such a way that its truth is radiated by its words, does for the class an effective service.

We have already shown how by a voluntary mental act we can recall a thing once well known, by training the mind to proceed methodically in its search for that which has for the moment escaped us, bringing to mind systematically the places, times, and circumstances with which it may possibly have been associated. Thus we may aid ourselves in recalling a truth by locating it in its Bible home, associating it with the book and the writer. He who knows the residence of a text, so to speak, who is familiar with the externals of each book in the Bible, who can readily analyze each book, knows how to proceed with his search for a given text, knows the limited number of places where such a text can be found, knows who would be liable to write it, in what connection he would be likely to write it, etc. He who accustoms himself to recall truth thus systematically soon has a surprising command of the Bible.

The teacher should make a special effort to train the pupil thus to familiarize himself with every section of the Bible, so that he can with ease trace every truth home.

The art of remembering words must not be regarded as the highest art. Many have the power of verbal memory who have no great mental ability. Indeed, it may almost be said to be a dangerous art to develop, if it go no farther. It is one of the early phases of memory, and is to be employed to great advantage between the ages of seven and twelve or fifteen. Soon after the child begins to memorize words he should be trained to remember truth independently of the words in which it is expressed.

Here the Bible excels all other books in adaptability to the development of the human mind. It not only has an indefinite array of clear, simple, beautiful texts that can be memorized and utilized, regardless of their surroundings, sentences that have not their equal in any other book, but it has a beautiful array of incidents, the language of which one could scarcely remember if he would, but the thought of which is retained with great ease, — such as the parables, miracles, and historical incidents.

There is as definite and clear a demand for teaching to memorize incidents divorced from the expression, as there is for memorizing words, and, in a sense, a greater demand for it.

A fish takes air through its gills so long as the water keeps the gills open, but no longer; so some people remember a truth so long as the words in which it floats keep the mind limbered up, but never think of it, pant for it in vain until they can get the first word of the text, and then it all comes back to them. Important as is the remembrance of words in their place, it is as important to remember truth without attempting to fix the words. If we cannot do that, we are mentally weak and should strengthen that faculty.

The next higher grade of this art is power to

remember truth that is not clothed in incident or story. In Job we find great truths grandly stated, but the truth is powerful aside from the language, and is best remembered without it. Many truths in the prophecies are of the same order. The truth is clear and grand, and, as truth, needs to be remembered.

Higher yet is the art of remembering truth in its relations to life and other truth. That touches God and man at the same time with a closely affiliating power. For illustration, Rom. 4: 13: "For the promise, that he should be the heir of the world, was not to Abraham, or to his seed, through the law, but through the righteousness of faith." There is no occasion to remember this text. Its language is not calculated to cling tenaciously to the mind, and there is no incident to fix the truth. The truth itself is forcible, that Abraham's faith in God's promises, rather than his obedience to the law, made him heir to all that his seed have inherited. The Epistles are full of truths that need to be lifted above their language and incidents, and be remembered in their dissociated grandeur as the essence of truth.

One of the most important elements in the art of remembering Bible truths is to discriminate what is to be remembered and how it is to be remembered. To commit those texts whose rhythm and truth are companionable is safe, because all such texts are serviceable. There is not a text in the entire Word of God, that is adapted to easy memorizing, that is not valuable, and there is not a truth that we need to have crystallized in harmonious phrase that is not so set in some text. The key to success lies in wasting neither time nor energy, making no false move. There is time to teach all that needs to be taught, provided it be well done.

Another indispensable element in the art of remembering is to awaken a deep, permanent interest in Bible truth. A young lady has no difficulty in remembering a stitch in fancy work, a shade of ribbon, or a style of lace, who cannot possibly remember the golden text. A housewife will remember with ease a recipe that a gentleman wouldn't attempt for anything, but she cannot memorize the simplest text. A lad will remember all the details of a game of base ball that would be an impossibility to a college professor, but he declares that he cannot learn Scripture. If we can awaken an interest in the Bible, if we can by any device, fervency, or tact make children love the texts and truths they learn, it will supplement all methods with a power above and beyond them.

PHILOSOPHY OF HABIT.

"For use almost can change the stamp of nature."
— SHAKESPEARE.

"Patient continuance in well-doing." — ROM. 2 : 7.

"Continue in prayer." — COL. 4 : 2.

"Habit is an internal principle which leads us to do easily, naturally, and with growing certainty, what we do often." — WEBSTER.

CHAPTER V.

PHILOSOPHY OF HABIT.

WE have accustomed ourselves to apply the term "habit" only to the vicious tendencies of mind and body. We are liable to forget that in the true sense and under proper restrictions it is an important means of conserving mental energy. Our faculties have an inherent tendency, when left to themselves, to form wrong habits of actions, so that people, naturally refined, are safe only when they have established correct modes of activity.

Medical science and surgical skill are teaching us what may be done in righting physical deformities, adjusting many bodily ills that were supposed unchangeable. Mankind is indebted, beyond its power to repay, to the thought and experiment that have made these physical changes possible.

The mind is infinitely more susceptible to

modifying influences, good or bad, than the body. While the body is an organism of growth, the mind is largely one of development. Mental deformities are rebellions, to be quelled or coerced by the rectifying activities of the mind.

Our manners, conduct, and behavior are the resultants of physical and mental tendencies and influences, under the direction of duty or obligation. Our religious thoughts and emotions are the Heavenward tendencies of the intellect and feelings under what seems to be Divine guidance. We consider habit, then, as physical, moral, intellectual, or religious.

In the strict sense, habit applies to those acts that are under the control of the will. Its aim and tendency for good or ill are to reduce the will-element to the minimum, so that we may do right or wrong without drawing upon the will. Habit establishes a disposition to do a certain thing in a given way under specified conditions, without appreciable motive or effort.

After anything has been done in one way repeatedly, we come to do it without noticeable attention, unactuated by any recognized desire, purpose, or resolve. This condition is attainable, physically, morally, mentally, or religiously, through frequent, uniform repetition of voluntary operations until they are performed as well involuntarily, and, so far as any mental exhaustion is concerned, unconsciously. Habit, therefore, practically creates brain power and nerve energy, performing acts and accomplishing results which naturally draw upon the mind and will without the exercise of any measurable mental or nerve force.

Ice-cutters will take a pond on which the ice is two feet thick and more, and by grooving the surface an inch or two will crack it into cakes with no appreciable effort. So our lives are blocked out for years by the grooves which habit runs in youth.

We will consider chiefly the influence of habit for good, since the best way to prevent or rectify a bad habit is to establish, through direct effort of the will, its antidote, good habit. The power of habit, physically considered, may be illustrated by the habit of early rising. A man has a strong inclination to indulge in the luxury of an extended morning nap. For convenience of the family, from business interest, or out of self-respect, he decides to yield to that disposition no longer. It requires a great effort of the will at first; after a little time the effort required is lessened, until, if he never wavers, he will put his physical nature into a new line of action. The time required depends upon the age and strength of the old habit; but, under any circumstances, the will can adapt the system to the new regime. There must be sufficient determination, an unwavering constancy in the exercise of the new habit.

This illustrates the true method of dealing with all physical habits. To break up the habit of intemperance or any kindred vice, we must form a habit of total abstinence. There needs to be an all-mastering decisiveness in the initiative act, as there was in the case of early rising. The will needs to give its entire attention to the decisive act, and then it needs to bend all its energies to total abstinence, regardless of the amount of will power required, until the physical system habituates itself to the new order of things.

In the case of physical habits, where the aim

is to establish a habit of utter disregard of certain sense-appeals or physical craving, much depends upon the reasons and motives for forming the new habits. These may be so great, and the good to be attained may come home to the mind with such vividness, that the habit may be as good as formed instantly. Some of the almost miraculous reforms of the intemperate under Mr. Moody's leadership are psychologically explained in this way.

That the true way to break up a vicious habit is to form another good habit will be apparent to anyone who will consider the matter in its relation to the action of the mind.

As we shall show in the chapter on Emotion, it is possible to cure even organic diseases of some kind by a change of the thought, directing the attention elsewhere, while it is well-nigh impossible to get remedies to act, if the patient studies his own symptoms.

Change of attention is absolutely essential for the remedy of a bad habit. When one says continually, "I will not do it. I will not, will not do it," it is simply a question of time how long before he will do it. Every time he says he will *not* do it, he rivets his attention upon it, and is, to a certain extent, magnetized by the fascination of it. If, on the contrary, he can fix his attention upon doing something else, he is making the permanency of his reform certain.

When an intemperate man reforms, he stands a hundred times as good a chance of holding firm to his changed life if he keeps clear of all temperance work and goes into church work as a general Christian laborer. The true idea of temperance reform is not reached, and will not be until the church gathers individually the men who need to be reformed, and keeps them active in Christian work not associated with thoughts of their past.

This necessity is illustrated in the home where a shrewd mother — and mothers need to know the philosophy of psychology — cares for her children.

A child hurts himself: one mother will pick him up and pet and kiss him, and soothe the "bumped" head, keeping the child's thought on it longer than he otherwise would. We have seen children, after falling, look around to see if they can see the mother; if not, they go on with their play without more ado; but if they can see the shadow of the mother, they rush to her for the luxury of tears and "coddling."

Another and wiser mother will not touch the child unless the injury be serious, will not appear to notice that any accident has happened, but will, with tact, turn the child's thought from himself and from his accident.

The secret of success in all change of habit from bad to good is to get the current of thought changed.

Habitual indifference to everything that does not contribute to our good is a necessity. The artist trains himself to habitual indifference to everything but the ideal in his landscape. The sculptor works away at a block of shapeless marble, indifferent to all but the ideal image seen only by himself.

The man who would attain unto perfect manhood must learn to be habitually indifferent to the invitations that tempt to anger, to the vexations that prompt to jealousy, to the social gossip that breeds envy. No character is well formed that is not founded on habitual indifference to every external influence. This must be cultivated with the same decision and persistency of purpose that any other habit is. It yields to the same laws.

Morality is conformity to the highest standard of right and virtuous action, with the best intention founded on principle.

Circumstanced as we are, it requires a vigorous exercise of the will, strong mental energy, to be moral in this sense, but such habits may be formed that we shall promptly and uniformly choose to abide by the highest rules of morality without appreciable effort.

An attempt has been made to discount such virtue as meritless because requiring no struggle. There are different degrees of disposition to virtue as to vice, but the rule holds that no one attains this condition of apparently automatic virtue until he has had so many self-conquests as to make resistance to temptation so natural as to be done unconsciously. These conquests may have been so early in life, this habit may have been formed at such an early age, that virtue is practically ingrained, making its possessor in the highest sense cultured in the art of morality. Such virtue is of the choicest variety.

Religion concerns the thoughts, emotions, and actions of man in his relation to God. Man may be religious by so exercising the will as to place and hold himself in an attitude toward the triune Deity, which is at once reverent, obedient, and affectionate. This religious attitude becomes permanent through an established habit. It is a mistake to content ourselves with the first choice of Christ and consequent joy of reliance on him. Our faith, hope, and love must develop into habitual activity.

Before we allow ourselves to form religious habits there should be an intelligent, affectionate choice of Christ as our Lord and Saviour. If we do not start right in the religious life, if we allow our habits to form on any other than an intelligent principle, we shall find ourselves encumbered with habits, to uproot which will require time and immense will-power. It will threaten to break up the very foundations of our belief. It is a dangerous experiment to teach a child to fear and serve the Lord from superstition rather than intelligent love. It is a mistake to teach anybody to view God as content with the observance of any special ceremonies, or the acceptance of any eccentricity of belief. It is inexcusable in this age of the world to estimate God's satisfaction with our belief or worship by a certain delectable, emotional state into which we may acquire the art and habit of working ourselves.

Any one of these errors is liable to make a man an intense disciple on false lines, magnifying stubbornness into grace, fanaticism into courage, and erratic, mischief-making tendency into a virtue.

A believer in Christ, who consecrates his life to the Master without intelligent, balanced instruction in the formation of correct habits of belief, emotion, and activity, is a prey to a variety of evil tendencies.

If in the formation of habits there be such infrequency that the effect of one effort passes away before a second is made, no number of these distant performances will effect a habit.

Every single mental act spends its energy after a definite season as certainly as any mechanical or physical force. In order to keep the mind and heart in such a state of activity that a habit is formed, the early repetitions must be frequent.

Uniformity is equally essential. An act may be performed nine times in ten; but if it be varied or omitted the tenth time, it vitiates all the others. In any good habit the virtue lies in constant uniformity of right-doing. There is the highest psychological philosophy in the text that teaches that he who offends in one point is guilty of all.

To be a Christian, and enjoy all the privileges and rewards that it implies, is to make intelligent choice of Christ, to rely affectionately upon him, to serve him with such frequency of act and uniform loyalty of devotion as to make our Christian thought, emotion, and choice a permanent habit.

USE OF THE IMAGINATION.

"Let none of you imagine evil against his brother." — ZECH. 7 : 10.

"Imagination rules the world." — NAPOLEON.

"Imagination consists in taking parts of our conceptions and combining them into new forms and images more select, more striking, more delightful, more terrible, etc., than those of ordinary nature."

— WEBSTER.

"Keep this forever in the imagination of the thoughts of the heart of thy people." — 1 CHRON. 29 : 18.

CHAPTER VI.

USE OF THE IMAGINATION.

A CHILD becomes in large measure what his imagination inspires him to be. A father may be the essence of truth and righteousness, the mother the embodiment of devotion and affection, the teacher consecrated and faithful, the pastor sincere and eloquent, and yet, by the neglect of the child's imagination, leave others to determine what manner of man he shall be. Some older playmate, nurse, servant, hostler, or other companion, may steal a few minutes now and then to charge his mind with the wildest flights of imagination of the sea, of frontier life, of licentious possibilities, of heroic deeds, of cunning exploit; and that boy of many prayers may go from the best home into a profligate life. The broken-hearted parents, the disappointed teacher, the discouraged pastor cannot understand the wayward tendency of a child so well brought up. They do not appreciate the importance of wise training of the imagination. No child is safe, humanly speaking, whatever other good influences surround him, whose imagination is not directed by some intelligent, discriminating, magnetic, Christian mind.

The imagination, when properly developed, keeps from mischief on the one hand and develops virtue and faith on the other. In place of forcing a child to work, it is possible to give such an imaginative turn to his duties that he shall delight in them. Observe the mother who has tact with her children. She wants the yard cleared up by boys, and not one of them wants to work. Instead of requiring it of them, and spending her time in enforcing obedience, she quietly says, "Now play the door-yard was the Mechanics' Fair building, and the exhibition is advertised to open at three o'clock. Do you think it is in condition to receive Governor Robinson and his suite? Which department will you get ready, Joe? And you, Frank?" At once the yard is transformed, and they imagine themselves in the great building, and have a grand time clearing up, and are sorry when there is not a stone or stick left. She teaches them to make work light, and exercises the imagination in healthful ways.

Many scholarly men have been recreant in their loyalty to God, aye, even to the higher morality, because their imaginations have been stimulated along merely scholastic lines. As society is constituted, the Sunday-school teacher has the privilege of fashioning the future of the young through the best possible resources for christening the imagination.

Success depends upon determining the relative natural strength or weakness of this faculty in each child. In most children it is sufficiently marked in some direction. With one it is inventive, with another dramatic, with others emotional. There are cases in which it gives a keen sense of beauty, a higher appreciation of, and insight into, truth. It is the parent's first duty to discover the natural bent of the child's imaginative faculty, and estimate its strength for good or ill. The teacher is not under the same obligation and has not the same opportunities, but in a general way he can to advantage estimate the imaginative possibilities of the child.

In early life, and to a great extent through life, it is an involuntary mental exercise, and as such needs to be baited with a sincere, successful appeal to the interest, and, so far as the teacher knows the native bent of the child's mind, he can use such knowledge in awakening an interest in the higher processes.

The child's attitude of mind must be assumed by the teacher. The imagination must be fed upon that which is already known. Although it may make startling transformations in matters of size, shape, relations, and circumstances, it nevertheless develops through assimilation of what is known. The teacher is always tempted to use his own knowledge, and develop those phases of the imagination which he most enjoys.

It is of the utmost importance, therefore, that the teacher place himself in such confidential, friendly relations with the children that he may hear them express themselves freely upon subjects of their own choosing, in order that he may supplement his theory of what they ought to know by his observation of what they do know and in what they have a lively interest.

He needs to know what they imagine regarding themselves and their future; their relations to their inferiors, their equals, their superiors; their relation to God, to the authority of God's law in the Bible, and conscience.

The imagination idealizes that which is known into what they wish might be. It is to be taught to idealize it into what it *ought* to be. All knowledge may be transformed into an aid or a hindrance in life. It is the teacher's privilege to furnish those conditions which will give it a right bias, developing it into what it should be.

In accomplishing this, several things are essential, — (1) to appreciate what is already known, having it so clearly outlined, so ready for use, that any fact known will be at hand without searching for it; (2) to know what is attainable through its use, having clear conception of the possibilities of this faculty; (3) to understand how to attain that after which we aspire. This requires close attention to the method and manner of its use.

A motive must be established before there is a balance-wheel provided which assures any degree of safety. No human foresight can anticipate the consequences of creating an interest for the imagination without guarding and guiding it with a well-established motive.

Every idea, vital to the Christian life here and hereafter, needs to be vividly pictured. Little incidents in play-life, in school-life, in the workshop and home, need to be transformed through the imagination into victories, accomplishments, and attainments, through Christ. It is easy, as it is valuable, to train children to estimate in imagination the benefit to character that comes with being just to ourselves, our fellow men, and God.

In furnishing a motive, the teacher of the Bible has the advantage of all others, as he has in estimating the influence on character of every thought and act. The texts, parables, and allusions give imaginative views, or the materials for such views, of the consequences of action.

Imagination must be allowed all the play it demands, but it must be kept on the track of

Divine law, getting its exercise in onward movement rather than in skeptical speculations and vagaries. Loyalty to the Scriptures is nowhere more important than in imagination.

People whose imaginations have not been skilfully handled, who lack skill to break up experiences, and truths into sections, and regroup them on a broader scale, make that class in society that wants a belief to emphasize some one element of faith or worship. They want everything in earth and Heaven to depend upon some insignificant thing, some materialization of a theory, some tangible idea. The unbalanced, uncultured imagination provides erratic people who recruit the delusive and vicious "isms." Take any new semi-religious delusion with a curative attachment, and it is notorious that nearly every cranky, whimsical device to ruin the souls of men by too much or too little religion has a healing art attached to it, and it will be found that almost every one whom it enlists has been previously "off" on some other kindred delusion. As a rule, it is psychologically demonstrable that their imagination lacks balance and culture. The philosophy of it is, that those whose imaginative powers are accustomed to magnify one idea in faith or practice are constantly contracting that faculty, and can only be satisfied with an ever-increasing fanaticism to meet the requirements of a disordered imagination. In due time nothing that is sound in sense or reliable in philosophy will or can gratify them. The teacher who trains pupils so that they shall escape such snares does them and the world a service.

A well-trained imagination gives power to estimate correctly present acts in their future relations; in other words, their personal, social, and religious consequences for good or evil, for time and eternity. No other book offers such facility for developing the mind in this regard as the Bible, and the teacher can readily use it in such a way as to establish a habit of thought by which it can know and experience truth, and gain facility in developing such keen and reliable imaginative power that in each event of life he instinctively pictures the possible and probable results of each of two available choices. Then it is easy to establish right principles of action.

THE EMOTIONS.

> "Some feelings are to mortals given
> With less of earth in them than heaven."
> — SCOTT.

"Thinking is only a dream of feeling." — NOVALIS.

"To maintain a flow of pleasure is the highest consummation of vital energy." — BAIN.

VII.

THE EMOTIONS.

THERE are two classes of feelings which do not come legitimately under the head of emotions. All the susceptibilities due to the putting forth of muscular energy are classed as muscular feelings; while those due to the action of the outer world upon us through the senses are styled sensations.

Emotions, properly considered, are less definite, less tangible. They are secondary and complicated, the diffused effect of a variety of causes physical and mental.

The emotions act through the nervous system upon the various bodily organs. The face first and most naturally expresses the emotions. It does this involuntarily, and yet we may so train the countenance, may make the facial muscles and nerves so pliable and responsive, that the expression may be more prompt to voice, in its glow, the fervor of the emotions.

One of the most efficient teachers of elocution makes it a prominent feature of his instruction to have the muscles and skin of the face made so flexible, so free and responsive, that what is read or spoken shall express itself involuntarily in the countenance. We have seen persons under such instruction who acquired ability to make not only the cheeks but the forehead radiant with emotion.

There is direct physical connection between the emotions and the digestive organs. Many of the phenomenal cures reported as the result of mental or "Christian" science, are resultants of skilful use of the emotions upon those organs. People with great personal magnetism, either natural or acquired, will stimulate faith so as to get the thought entirely divorced from self, from the body. They will awaken hope which quickens every emotional avenue. They will quicken this into joy, or the exuberance of spirits. All this time the thought is kept away from self. Then, when the emotional power is at its height, it is suddenly turned back upon self with such a commanding tone as to make it a joyful servant, is concentrated upon the stomach with the assurance that nothing is the matter with it,—that it only needs food and enough of it. There are well-authenticated cases where people's digestive organs, long deranged, had reached a condition that medicine offered no promise of relief, and this summary treatment produced definite and continued relief.

The heart, the lungs, and the kidneys are directly reachable by the emotions.

It is a discredit to the science of medicine, philanthropy, and Christianity that beneficial influences of the emotions should have been so far left undeveloped that those who are no credit to Christianity, or are direct opponents thereof, can avail themselves of its power to our disadvantage.

Those who under-estimate the importance of emotional self-control do themselves and those whom they influence a definite wrong. Even the injury that comes to people socially from ill manners, bred by lack of emotional balance, is greater than may be supposed. We all know those who, when asked a question, scratch their heads, shrug their shoulders, close their eyes, or do some other unmannerly thing, all from lack of emotional self-control.

We know those who are always beating time with the foot, or tapping out a tune with the fingers on the slightest provocation, as though so full of music that they cannot control it. The fact is that such persons have not command of their musicael motions, so to speak.

Trained musicians, those who by voice or instrument thrill the world with cultured art, have such control of their musical emotions that they husband all that fervor for occasions when it will be effective.

The entire physical system is largely under the sway of the emotions. All pleasurable emotions conserve physical energy, tend to restore health, and prolong life.

Painful emotions, on the other hand antagonize physical energy, tend to disease and death. There is no way in which to define either pleasure or pain. We know the emotions, but to state in words that which we know is, in this case, not easy. They are, in all senses, direct opposites. The one is headed toward life, the other toward death.

Human conduct is largely dependent upon the emotions. Pleasure stimulates us to physical and mental activity. Pain tends to caution and inactivity. With a large portion of mankind you can estimate their emotional nature in quality and quantity by their choices and conduct.

Right conduct relies for constancy upon a properly adjusted emotional fervor. Contentment and enjoyment in life depend in great measure upon the development and discipline of the emotions.

Without the stimulus of emotion, man may be good in a tame way. Without control of the emotions, he is a candidate for irretrievable ruin. Stimulated but unrestrained emotions rush those who began life with the best intentions, into drunkenness, licentiousness, skepticism, or infidelity.

Excessive emotional natures need restraint. There is an exuberance of feeling which leads to an over-estimate of everything good or ill, to too great intensity in likes and dislikes.

Erratic emotional natures need to be modified. Many of the crooked, caustic, notional beings who afflict home, church, and society, are what they are from emotional deformities. The man with a hump-back, club-feet, or any other physical deformity is a lesser monstrosity than the man or woman whose emotional nature is deformed in such a way as to make him unreliable in friendship, fickle in interest, rasping in manner.

Success in study is largely dependent upon the way in which the lesson, the teacher, and the surroundings appeal to the emotions.

It is important to note the tendency of feelings, observing the class of influences that most readily affect them, and their effect upon the thought and conduct.

While all natures need appropriate emotional development, those dull natures need to be specially stimulated. In all cases, however, excessive emotional stimulant is to be rigidly avoided. Pleasure results from certain excitants, and the unscientific instructor presses these supposed advantages beyond the proper limit, producing evil rather than good results. For instance, the teacher learns that he can give pleasure to his pupils by exciting their love of rivalry through medals and prizes. He may intensify their zeal until he makes them emotionally miserable through envy and bitterness of feeling. He will, if not careful, cause them to carry this so far as to make them lose all love for study, making them envious of each other and suspicious of his fairness. All this may easily result from excessive emotional stimulant.

Too long continuance of any pleasurable emotion is unfortunate, since, in the nature of a stimulant, its merit consists in its being frequently relieved, so that its good effects may be assimilated and matured.

After each application of a stimulant there must be time given for the return of a perfectly natural condition, and fresh strength must be supplied for the stimulant to quicken. So long as the excitant calls into activity superabundant force that else would be unemployed, all is well; but when it rallies to action forces that are needed in other departments, or whose time of action has not arrived, it is mischievous.

A tree, after a season's growth, sheds its

leafage because the leaf-stems are no longer large enough for the enlarged branch, hence they are laid aside, and the branch seasons into its increased size, and firmly knits its fibre, and puts forth a wholly new set of leaves for a re-enlargement. By this process the tree grows.

There is a phase of medical science that seeks to give, in most diseases, the least medicine that will stimulate healthy action, and then awaits the accomplishment of its effect before re-applying the remedy.

Thus the emotional life, and all faculties of mind and heart dependent upon it, need to rest after every emotional stimulant, for its work to be accomplished and its results established in habitual activity.

The sympathetic teacher errs when he exhausts his nervous energies in an attempt to hold the attention and interest of the pupils by incessant appeals to their emotional nature. If, in place of this, he would appeal to their feelings for a definite purpose, then rest himself, and study the effect of that exertion, his effort would go further, accomplish more, and he would avoid exhaustion. The aim should be to so use appeals to pleasure as to put the entire system in a healthy, elastic state, prompting to the best activity. It wants to exert such influence over the other faculties that they shall work in full sympathy with the emotions, but not be dependent upon them.

Those who depend upon their feelings to decide what they shall do, when they shall do it, and how long continue it, are inevitably unhappy and miserable most of their time. No business suits them, and, after the new is off, they do everything in a state of fretfulness, chafing under every requirement, rasped by their superiors, envious of their equals, jealous of their inferiors. They seek relief in change of occupation, always looking for something they feel like doing. Each change makes contentment and pleasure shorter-lived.

Thus the undisciplined emotional nature is responsible for much of the shiftlessness and thriftlessness, intemperance and licentiousness, homesickness and heartsickness of the world.

It is the privilege, as well as duty of the

Bible teacher to so use the Scripture remedies with psychological wisdom as to give balance and tone to the feelings that they may be restrained from doing evil and be made effective for good. All this will help to furnish a better developed physical and mental nature in which to nurture the religious life.

Erratic, unreliable, professed followers of Christ, who have at one time been sincere seekers after the assurance of forgiveness, but have never persisted in the performance of religious duties, are usually of that class who seek Heaven on their feelings. Those who run hither and thither after every fanatic, who incline to every peculiar theory for healing disease without science, who advocate every phase of philanthropy and reform that has no philosophic basis, advertise the fact that they have left their emotional faculties untrained. Those who adopt every new "ism" in theology, who never enjoy their religion except in a revival, are of the same unfortunate class of undirected and uncontrolled emotional natures.

The Word of God, judiciously, intelligently applied, is the essence of virtue in balancing the emotions so as to stimulate every faculty of mind and heart. At the same time it tones down every excitable, fickle, clamorous emotion by harmonizing conflicting hopes and fears, doubts and aspirations. It does this through a restful confidence in and reliance upon the triune Deity for love, peace, and joy. The Bible and its truth may be so taught that nothing in earth can permanently go amiss with him who confides affectionately in God. It can give assurance that our Heavenly Father holds in his hands all possibilities of matter and mind. It can inspire us to seek and hope for perfect emotional satisfaction through the truth of God and its Author.

PHILOSOPHY OF SYMPATHY.

"We pine for kindred natures
To mingle with our own."
— MRS. HEMANS.

"A mystic bond of brotherhood makes all men one." — CARLYLE.

"The secrets of life are not shown except to sympathy and likeness." — GEORGE ELIOT.

"The craving for sympathy is the common boundary-line between joy and sorrow." — HARE.

"Sympathy is especially a Christian's duty." — SPURGEON.

"Those who would make us feel must feel themselves."
— CHURCHILL.

CHAPTER VIII.

PHILOSOPHY OF SYMPATHY.

SYMPATHY leads all the beneficent emotions as a power in the hands of the teacher. There is no sphere in life in which one may not be more effective in steadying the wayward, in comforting the sorrowful, in winning souls to permanent love for the Lord and constancy in his service by judicious, fervent use of the sympathetic emotions.

There is a physical sympathy which is almost purely mechanical and involuntary. Evidence of this may be seen in a public audience, where one has a cough and all about desire to cough from sympathy. Laughter and yawning exhibit the same physical tendency.

It is not for display merely that soldiers are trained to keep step, but there is physical gain, —a certain added energy in having a battalion step in unison. A thousand men will endanger a bridge less by walking out of step than five hundred will that keep step. When any number of people unite in a common physical movement, each puts a certain personality into it, and does it better and with more force than he would alone. Harmony is the essence of power as well as beauty.

Intellectually there is keener sympathy than physically. Those accustomed to address public audiences appreciate this. One or two strong minds in full sympathy with the speaker exert a magnetic influence, carrying conviction with their unvoiced intellectual loyalty. Contrariwise, a doubter or disbeliever can, without saying a word, create a strong intellectual opposition. Few characteristics of a speaker are so important as skill in bringing an audience into sympathy with his thought. Speakers who have a reputation for tact never enter upon their theme seriously until they have tested their audience with some experimental remark to assure themselves that they have the sympathy of their hearers. By these artful introductions speakers place their audiences in an intensified, sympathetic condition. Edward Everett was careful to have everything adjusted before he began an oration, that he might with greatest ease secure sympathy. A jury, unless it has one or two strong characters on it, has its judgment swayed very largely by the sympathy of the audience. Skilful lawyers advise their clients to have present as many friends of strong intellectual power as they can, for the direct benefit of a keen, sympathetic, intellectual atmosphere.

Mozart was so dependent upon sympathy that he could neither compose nor execute his musical compositions unless conscious that he was appreciated, or would be, by those to whom he was appealing.

Emotional sympathy is even more important. In the normal condition man reflects the feelings of others. The frolic or pain of animals sways our emotions when the mind is inactive.

When several pianos are in an uncarpeted room, if a given note be struck, that string will vibrate perceptibly in all the other instruments. Metallic picture-cords sometimes vibrate audibly when they chance to be attuned to a given key. The human heart is infinitely sensitive to the vibrations of others' joys and sorrows.

The will has its laws of sympathy as well as the physical, intellectual, and emotional natures. When we make no special effort to direct the thoughts and feelings, we reflect the decisions of those about us and act from sympathy with them.

This analysis of the departments of sympathy culminating in the influence it has over our choice, shows how important an element it is in human society. It enters into the feelings of others, and acts upon them as though they were our own. It is a universal force and must be properly provided for.

Not all use this power for the good of their fellow men. It is, relatively, as great a source of evil as of good. It is the strongest social force employed in wrecking virtue or debasing with intemperance. A young person whose sympathies are not given a virtuous, ennobling tendency is a candidate for the malarial influence of evil.

Those amusements upon which the church looks suspiciously have their mischievous tendency in this channel. Why does the church frown upon dancing, such a beautiful exercise, teaching grace of movement and social etiquette; upon the theatre, that tones up elocution, and emphasizes, oft-times, moral virtues? They, and kindred amusements, misdirect the sympathies. They provide the young with the wrong conditions. A person of strong will, or one who is egotistical or selfish, may be safe, but the great majority take serious risks.

If a jury sitting in judgment upon a man's life, with a discreet judge to preside, is liable to be affected by the sympathetic atmosphere of the court-room, how much more a bevy of lads and lassies, with no wise monitor. The ball-room appeals to the physical sympathies by whirling the nerves and the physical being into a state of unnatural excitement.

There is no premium on intellectual activity, but he who has given most attention to the physical graces with the fervor and glow acccompanying them is the most commanding in his influence over the sympathies. The conditions are ripe, and if there be one person who is not virtuous, whose mind runs in unchaste lines, whose emotions are wrong, his presence instinctively plays upon the sympathies of the impressible company.

In the theatre the auditor is passive, receptive, the mind and the emotions are relaxed. The will is free and easy. If, in a congregation or lyceum audience, one person who disbelieves can exert a perceptible prejudicial influence, what can be expected under the conditions existing in the theatre? If there be any considerable number present whose moral character is suspicious, whose thought is not elevating, their influence upon others will be debasing, would be if the same number, of the same character, were together, even in a church. If the scenery and costumes are questionably suggestive, if the character of the actors is questionable, then there is a circuit of most unfortunate conditions. Because a few strong-minded, self-willed people can take their recreation this way, is no reason others should tempt their sympathies. People of unformed characters certainly have no right to do so. "Evil communications corrupt good manners."

The very word "amusement" is prejudicial, testifying against itself. It appeals to selfishness. It offers to amuse those who wish to be thus catered to. Its object is to lull the faculties, prevent reflection, banish memories. "Entertainment" is better, because it indicates a willingness to enter into the activities. It awakens the mind, arouses the sensibilities. Recreation seeks a mere temporary suspension of activities preparatory to better labor. It is a cessation of activities for a purpose. It keeps the aim up to its old standard. It consents to relaxation, but not to diversion.

In every employment, whether of vocation or avocation, we need to have the thought sharply on the sympathies, their susceptibility, the quality and strength of the modifying influences. On this ground the church is a profitable place for any one to be. If no word be remembered, if no thought attach itself to the mind, positive benefit may accrue. The sermon, the Scripture, the prayer, and the hymns, one or all, exert a healthful influence through the sympathies. The majority of those present are there for good. They say a mental "Amen" to every good thought. They regret all lapses in the past. They resolve to be more correct and fervent in the future. They are hopeful and inspiring. Thus each finds himself in the best possible receptive attitude, and all the active forces are of a desirable quality. There is a philosophic argument for keeping the best company, and young people, especially, should be made to understand this philosophy.

There is a distinction between passive and active sympathy. The former merely feels *with* another. It is a contagious emotion, absorbing his mental state, reflecting his condition, vibrating with his sensibilities. Active sympathy feels for and acts with another, anticipating and endeavoring to satisfy his necessities. It enters into hearty alliance as a clarifying, rectifying, modifying force.

There is variety in sympathy. Sorrow, pain, affliction, and adversity call forth a quality of sympathy quite in contrast with that called for by pleasure, prosperity, and joy. Few fail of a tender sensibility when their fellow men, or even animals, suffer. It is exceptional that one hesitates to feel or express sorrow even when an enemy suffers. But when people are successful, circumstances change. The human heart is predisposed to envy under such conditions. John the Baptist reached a high plane of spiritual self-command when he could say with apparent relish, "He must increase, but I must decrease."

To rejoice with those who rejoice is a more refined emotion than to weep with those who weep, and prepares for the highest grade of sympathy with those in need. It indicates a more signal victory over our rebellious, jealous, envious natures.

We mistake seriously when we think of sympathy as merely interest in those who are afflicted, sorrowful, and suffering. Too many thus confine their thought to that phase of it which weights us with others' woes, which leads the heart to ache because other hearts ache. We must remember, as we have remarked, that it is in some respects a better, keener phase which blends ourselves with others in their interests, whether they be joyful or sorrowful.

The organ has its couplers by which the various banks of keys and departments may be connected. It is the work of a moment to draw the register, after which the touching of a pedal-note gives that note in the great organ, and in the swell also. Sympathy is such a coupling in human minds and human interests.

There is a closeness of interest between minds that are in sympathy that merges them in a common power. When officers, teachers, and scholars have such sympathy, they will learn more with less friction than they otherwise will. If you will try to sound a given note unaided, and will then sit before an expert elocutionist or musician, and sound it with him, you will find that his voice rounds out and fills out yours; you can sound the note much easier, and it will be richer and more resonant. It is, as it were, an alliance of voices, which, without effort, melodizes both. Thus, people who are mutually sympathetic round out each other's experiences and characters.

The instinctive, momentary, sympathetic feeling for one in sorrow or joy has little virtue in it. It signifies nothing of moral value unless it abides with us. It must represent our pain or pleasure. It must affect and direct our will as well as our emotion. The measure of virtue in our sympathy is our activity in relieving pain or augmenting pleasure. We test sympathy through the activity in which it eventuates.

Sympathy for which one has to ask is never satisfactory. We need, therefore, to train ourselves in the habit of appreciative attention to the slightest indications of the unvoiced emotions of others.

This sympathy, however spontaneous it may appear, needs cultivation. There are many ways in which it may be abused. For instance, the mental phenomenon known as mesmeric sleep is a simple device by which one acquires the art of practically closing all avenues of thought and emotion but one, concentrating all the sensibilities on that one line of sympathy with some one person, through memory or imagination. Such an act throws innumerable possibilities into one channel. Under these conditions the sympathies are profuse and intense, but unbalanced and unreliable. This shows the possibilities of misuse of this faculty.

In the best sense, sympathy is one of the higher phases of the emotional life, and increases strength and improves the quality the higher the grade of intellect. There is a popular sentiment which discounts this claim. There is a certain reserve, dignity, unapproachableness in some prominent intellectual characters that has given the impression that the keener the intellectual training the lower and less responsive the sympathy. This merely proves the possibility and shows the danger of developing the intellect away from the sympathy. It does not prove that such development is natural. It indicates lack of mental poise, however acute the thought, if the sympathy wanes as mental culture increases.

Awakening the senses awakens the sympathies. Appeals to the lower range of sensibilities arouse the sympathies that tend wrongfully, while those which quicken the finer sensibilities develop the better sympathies. This explains the availability of the song-service in revivals. Those songs that appeal to a low range of emotions frequently stimulate a false hope in Christ and produce erratic disciples. It is better to use those nobler hymns, those standard melodies that have a true sentiment, that teach the higher range of sympathies.

Whoever is unduly occupied with his own affairs shuts out the experiences of others, so that he cannot receive or reflect them, cannot benefit or be benefited by them.

Whoever demands that others come to his level, who views everything from his own standpoint, loses the comfort of sympathy or the power to comfort through it. Such a tendency develops the selfish, egotistical, unshareable elements in our nature. Whoever enjoys rivalry and competition, through his energies, wherever there is opportunity to excel, simply from love of victory, soon precludes the possibility of being genuinely sympathetic with men in their need.

The oyster builds his shell so that the inside is smooth as pearl, but the outside is rough, coarse, unsightly, unattractive. Thus non-sympathetic people seem to care only for polishing up circumstances and interests that come in contact with themselves, and by which they profit. It is a short-sighted policy. It is better every way to know by experience, in sympathy as well as in other things, that it is more blessed to give than to receive. It pays to smooth that which chafes others as well as ourselves.

Whoever trains himself by habit to criticise others loses the power to benefit himself or others through sympathy. Such an attitude of mind leads one to observe the manner, action, and speech with a view to discovering subjects for unfavorable comment, and he will make his estimate upon what he expected to see, and will be inclined to think he saw it even though he did not. The motive with which we look into others' actions largely determines what we see there.

> "Do not look for wrong and evil —
>   You will find them if you do;
>
> "Look for goodness, look for gladness,
>   You will meet them all the while;
> If you bring a smiling visage
>   To the glass, you meet a smile."

Much depends upon the class of men and influences with which we are in sympathy. We should aim to be in personal sympathy with the best men in our circle of acquaintances, in our nation, in our age, the best men in history.

Society, politics, theology, and the church itself, are always liable to be in commotion. Parties arise, issues are made, and much depends upon our attitude in such emergencies. It is of the highest importance that we secure a reputation for being uniformly in sympathy with those men and measures which represent the most conscience and common sense.

It is well to emphasize that phase of Christianity which consists in being actively in sympathy with the needs of humanity; with the requirements of God's word in repentance, and all moral virtues; with all the privileges it offers through prayer, faith, and hope; with the personal Christ through confidential, experimental relations with him; with the Holy Spirit, in all his tender, comforting, inspiring ministration. That sympathy into which Christian experience introduces us is one of the most sacred emotions of the human heart.

Whoever wields the keenest, most judicious, sympathetic power will, other things being equal, most effectively and permanently mould character. He who commands the resources of Divine truth, the melody of Scripture texts, the enkindling fervor of the Holy Spirit, the compassionate love of Christ, has influences to awaken sympathy of the highest order. With this privilege comes corresponding responsibility.

According to the latest and most approved science, the teacher of deaf mutes, when she wishes the earless, voiceless child to read words from the lips of others, mechanically articulating the response, takes both the child's hands in her own, placing them upon either side of her body where the vibrations are most distinct, pressing them gently while speaking slowly, resonantly, that the sensitive touch of the child may aid in reading the vocal utterances of the lips through her eloquent form that vibrates rhythmically with her unheard voice.

Thus the Sunday-school teacher who adds to other qualities as an instructor that of sympathy will impart the thrill of Christian life and love from his vibrant life of truth as it is in Christ. He must remember to teach by precept as well as example, that the pupils whom he sends forth into life may perpetuate his power through the sympathies of mankind.

THE PHILOSOPHY OF BELIEF.

"What ardently we wish we soon believe." — YOUNG.

"Who never doubted, never half believed." — BAILEY.

"Uncertain ways unsafest are." — DENHAM.

"Believe on the Lord Jesus Christ, and thou shalt be saved."
— ACTS 16 : 31.

"Belief consists in accepting the affirmations of the soul."
— EMERSON.

"When in God thou believest, near God thou wilt certainly be."
— LELAND.

"The practical effect of a belief is the real test of its soundness."
— FROUDE.

"Doubt indulged soon becomes doubt realized." — HAVERGAL.

IX.

THE PHILOSOPHY OF BELIEF.

THE teacher of God's Word has the privilege and the duty of anchoring the mind and heart of humanity in all that is true and noble, hopeful and helpful, through an intelligent, restful belief in that which is eternal in its inspirations and rewards.

Anti-Christian writers, by their indifference to the claims of Christian truth, exert a disastrous influence upon many thoughtful youth who go from our instruction into the higher institutions of learning, or become readers of a class of aristocratic periodicals. The corrective of this impulse to doubt is such a judicious development of the art of believing, as shall enable the mind to weigh intelligently, honestly, and devoutly all literary criticism.

Discrimination in the use of terms is nowhere more vital than in estimating the relative merit and demerit of skeptical and devout views of human tendency and need, and divine power and truth.

Belief is prompt assent to or acceptance of that which we do not know with absolute certainty.

If we are absolutely certain that a fact is established or a proposition truthful from personal observation, experiment, or experience, then it is knowledge or belief crystallized.

There is a moral certainty in belief. In a sense, we are as sure that our belief is correct as of many things that we know by observation. I know that every object that I have ever seen, unsupported, falls to the earth. I believe that every object that is not properly supported will fall. I have no absolute knowledge that the apples that grow next year will fall to the ground if not otherwise gathered, but my belief that they will is as real and satisfactory to me as my knowledge, derived from the observations of this year.

When properly formed, belief is as reliable as knowledge, but it is radically different, and the distinction must not be lost sight of. Failure to appreciate this has led to serious mischief in many an experience.

It is a favorite device of those who would wreck the faith of humanity, to frighten men away from their belief because they are not absolutely certain of the truth which they believe. The man who understands what belief is, and appreciates that he rests it upon that which he absolutely knows, can meet all captious criticism as calmly as he would a denial that the sun will rise to-morrow — speaking after the manner of man — because we do not know that it will, we merely believe it.

It is also claimed by some anti-Christian men that it is a virtue not to give ready assent. This is the test: If we hesitate or waver, we do not believe. We may conclude or estimate that a thing is true after careful deliberation, but we only believe that which we assent to promptly.

He who knows his rights and privileges in belief occupies the same vantage ground as a man of business who is conversant with the written and unwritten laws that regulate mercantile affairs. There is no more reason why men should be imposed upon by the skeptic's sophistry than by a quack in medicine or a trickster in trade.

Belief makes all knowledge available. There is scarcely a thing which we know, that can be applied by us without belief. The doing of anything requires the projection of that which we know into the future, and that involves belief.

Science, art, and mechanics rest upon belief in the principles and laws of matter and force. Beyond the known is much to which we give prompt assent, and without which belief we could not progress in investigation or experiment.

Commercial and social relations have their security in belief in man, in his general loyalty to the principles of personal and public integrity and virtue.

Religion has as many known facts as its companions. It is not, as some would have us think, at a disadvantage in this regard. Man's necessities are known, his experiences are definite. The benefits of his prayers, faith, love, and worship, are matters of knowledge. Like all science, art, trade, and society, religion has its principles and laws to which the mind instinctively renders prompt assent. The belief of its votaries is as tangible and satisfactory, to say the least, as the belief of any other class of men in any department of life.

Belief is the normal attitude of the mind. We promptly accept the permanency of matter, constancy of force, and sincerity of man until we have experience with nature and life. There is no law, probably, so thoroughly established but that it has apparent exceptions sufficient to cause the child to hesitate in his loyalty, and this wavering condition of mind is doubt.

One who had never seen water except as a liquid, and had never heard of it in any other state, would believe that it is always thus. But on going to a climate in which it freezes, he would know that it is sometimes a solid, and all his belief concerning it would be shaken.

There are men, even preachers, among the negroes and mountain white people of the South who sincerely believe the earth to be flat and immovable until they are convinced that it is spheroidal, and both rotates and revolves.

This conviction destroys their former belief, and leads them to doubt the constancy of nature.

The child promptly accepts the fact of his mother's love because she feeds, cares for, and comforts him. His belief in her is instinctive until she declines to give him something that he desires; then he questions her love. He also accepts the fact of his father's love until he punishes him, and then the child challenges the father's claim. Doubt is the suspense of belief caused by discordant experiences.

So long as life moves in harmony with unquestioned belief all goes well; but one counter experience after nineteen favorable ones causes us to hesitate, and a repetition of this counter-experience leads us to readjust our theory; and this unsettled state of mind, in which we are uncertain whether we believe or not, is doubt.

Doubt is inevitable when circumstances favor. Indeed, it is a testimony, with some limitations, to a sound, healthy mind. The man who has never doubted anything may well question his own intelligence. Every belief has, practically, its period of doubt, which is not of necessity harmful.

The word *doubt* has been needlessly degraded. In its best sense it is like the soil in springtime, when it is being mellowed from frozen earth in preparation to germinate seed and be the depository of life. Under proper conditions, doubt is merely the pubescent state of belief.

It should be so utilized as to be a permanent assistance to belief. It needs to be used in tempering the belief to such elasticity that it will spring back from doubt into normal, confiding belief. The child who learns that the mother withheld the luxury for which he teased, to prevent pain and sickness, has ever after a higher type of belief in her love, though he may have doubted it when his wish was refused.

The father who hesitates to discipline his child, from fear that he will doubt his love, entirely mistakes the mission of doubt; he should even welcome the doubt, if in this way only he can be led to see the greater scope of his father's love.

The smith tempers steel to great elasticity by first heating it, and then dipping in water for an instant, repeating the process until it is properly tempered. If, however, he should plunge it in the water and leave it there, it would become too brittle for service. The scientific explanation seems to be that the gradual process gives the particles ability to cohere tenaciously to those on all sides.

So doubt, rightly used, seems to inspire us to keener intelligence in our search for the relations and foundations of our belief, and to more tenacious loyalty to beliefs that have been duly tempered. In this sense, "Who never doubted, never half believed."

> "There lives more faith in honest doubt,
> Believe me, than in half the creeds."

If we allow doubt to disintegrate our habit of belief, it will destroy all elasticity, and thus become disbelief.

Unbelief is doubt habituated. Disbelief is doubt enthroned. Unbelief neglects to accept truth; disbelief refuses to accept it. Disbelief is positive, aggressive, and denies belief. It is jealous of its authority, and will not be approached by any argument or evidence.

Doubt may be wise, unbelief may be merely heedless, but disbelief is normally a vicious state of mind. Doubt may lead to independence, unbelief may become remonstrance, disbelief is rebellion.

Disbelief leads to faintheartedness, apprehension of danger, fear of evil, alarm at every unexpected occurrence.

Despondency is a fruit of disbelief. It is permanent discouragement, and leads to the abandonment of effort to better our condition. It settles down to the work of life as to the inevitable, without heart. It is the end of intellectual activity, and may, perhaps, not inappropriately be styled the extreme of the evil of disbelief on the intellectual side of our being.

Despair is the extreme of the evil of disbelief from the emotional side. It is the height of horror, and bids farewell to hope and every comforting emotion. It companions with fear and remorse, and revels with them.

> "Of comfort no man speak:
> Let's talk of graves, of worms, and epitaphs."

This is the delirium tremens of the emotional life, brought on by the intoxication of disbelief when we drink overmuch of its evil.

Desperation is the extreme of the evil of disbelief on the volitional side of our being. It is disbelief despotically enthroned in the will, controlling the choices for its purpose, making the will do the bidding of despondency and despair.

> "O mischief! thou art swift
> To enter in the thoughts of desperate men."

The Sunday-school has not done its work until it has clearly taught the relation of doubt, unbelief, and disbelief, emphasizing the tendency of the latter, not fanatically, not as though its extremes were sure to follow, but as bearing a similar relation to disbelief that drunkenness bears to moderate drinking. Without placing involuntary doubt in a false position, we must arraign disbelief as a positive evil, personally, socially, and religiously.

Skepticism is a theological term whose full significance seems not to have been settled. It is used by different apparent authorities as referring to any one of the three states of mind, doubt, unbelief, or disbelief, and should be given the relative importance of the word for which it is used. Because of its vagueness, it is better to use one of the three terms whose significance is settled.

Any Christian leader, in pulpit or prayer-room, in the Sunday-school or home, who merely divides humanity into believers and unbelievers, who classes all who do not accept Christ as a personal leader in the same great company of sinners, takes a responsibility that may well cause him to shudder. To treat a doubter as though he were a disbeliever is to take the risk of outraging his better nature.

Disbelievers are more rare than we think. Our standard of profession and confession is not so perfected as to warrant any man in treating those who do not answer his interrogation as though he were a disbeliever. The very atmosphere has more faith in it than we give credit for. With all the laxity and heedlessness, with all the irreverence there is about us, there is not so much of disbelief after all. Frances Power Cobbe, in a recent number of the *Contemporary Review*, in speaking of the fact that the nearest approach to an atheist that we can produce is really no atheists at all, says, they " are no more fair samples of the outcome of atheism than a little party of English youths who had lived for a few years in Central Africa would be samples of negroes. It would take several thousand years to make a full-blooded atheist out of the scion of forty generations of Christians. Our whole mental constitutions have been built up on the food of religious ideas. A man on a mountain-top might as well resolve not to breathe the ozone in the air, as to live in the intellectual atmosphere of England and inhale no Christianity." Disbelief in a thorough Christian community is a difficult thing to mature. There is doubt, there is unbelief. There is danger of all the consequences we have been considering. We want to learn from Christ the art of winning the human mind and heart from doubt and unbelief to loyalty and allegiance.

Belief in its better phases is buoyant. As the bird fills its very bones with the air through which it flies, to give buoyancy to the body, so belief permeates the entire being, thrilling us with confidence in everything in earth and Heaven that God uses and would have us use. As the plumage of the bird partakes of the colors of the rainbow and the sunset, so, through belief, we may give to our earthly life the hue and tint of Heaven itself.

We should be honest with ourselves and our pupils, and admit that belief does not always tend to virtuous states of mind. We attempt too much when we assume to defend belief in all its phases and possibilities. It is too vast a subject, and ranges down the scale as well as up.

Credulity accepts promptly and with implicit confidence whatever appeals to our belief. The more improbable it is, the more enthusiastically it is believed. Gladstone speaks of credulity as the rival folly of excessive skepticism. It always brings sincere, intelligent belief into disrepute. Credulity, encouraged, leads to superstition on the one hand, or fanaticism on the other.

Superstition is the exercise of credulity along sombre lines. It leads to uncomfortable imaginings, weak fears, dark forebodings. It is allied with fatality. It is sordid, earthy, barbarous in its nature. It is antagonistic to intelligence, true virtue, and even civilization itself. It tends to superstitious reverence for signs and traditions, becoming in that way an almost criminal abuse of the privilege of believing.

The superstition in which we were brought up is said never to lose its power over us, even after we understand it. This is not strictly true, but it requires an immense waste of nerve energy and will power to rid ourselves of its grip. There are more than we suspect, among Christians even, who regard with more or less favor signs which have come down the generations. This exhibits the tenacity with which heathen idolatry clings to civilized life. Legitimate belief is discounted so long as those who exercise it dishonor God by suspecting him of being guilty of dealing with men, individually or collectively, by the whims of animals, by household accidents, or the chance of times or seasons. So long as God has all the resources of earth and Heaven through which to work, so long as He can speak directly to the human soul in mind or heart, so long as His Word speaks to the intellect and conscience of mankind, it is sacrilegious to study "signs" of coming mischief.

Fanaticism is an equally serious possibility in

the development of credulity, and is its aggressive tendency. It is self-confident assurance that we may rush madly into any course in which, in a high state of excitement, we believe, without regard to consequences. It leads to a conviction that we have a direct Divine guidance, which exempts us from all caution.

It regards expediency as a crime. To reason is akin to blasphemy, with the fanatic. The more solitary the believer in his fanaticism, the more certain he is that he is right. If he can only feel sure that there is not another person on earth who thinks as he does, his bliss is complete, as he abuses that glorious sentence, "One with God is a majority." There is no crime that fanaticism does not magnify into a virtue.

We cannot be too careful to disabuse the public mind of the impression that credulity, superstition, and fanaticism are the legitimate fruits of belief; neither can we be too definite in teaching youth that to it, weak, dangerous, and sometimes sinful tendencies may be given.

Expectant attention is another phase of belief to which we need to give thought. It is a term covering table-tipping, planchette, and kindred phenomena. It is called expectant attention because the whole mind is so possessed with the idea that a certain action will take place, and is "so eagerly directed towards the indications of its occurrence" with such emotional excitement as to produce, through involuntary muscular movement, the things they expect. The success of all the experiments here indicated require absolute faith and accompanying attention.

Dr. W. B. Carpenter has given special thought to these investigations, and his illustrations are invaluable aids.

It is a fact that some people with sufficient belief and power of attention can hold a ring suspended from the end of the finger near a glass tumbler, and have it swing against the tumbler until it has struck the hour of day. This has usually been accounted for as the work of "spirits," or supernatural influence. *When the performer is ignorant of the hour it will never strike the hour.* It is further noticeable that while in America it would strike *three* in the afternoon, in Italy it would strike *fifteen* according to the custom of the people.

There is no success unless the eye is fixed on the ring. It will not strike the glass with such regularity if the eyes are turned away. It requires belief, attention, and visual sense combined.

The turning of a hazel-fork when firmly held in both hands, as used in some country towns to point out the whereabouts of springs of water, is but another illustration of such belief or expectant attention. It will go up or down according to the way in which it is held: up, if the hands are nearer than the natural position of the forks; down, if farther apart. They will eventually move if we stand still as well as if we moved in search of water, and it will move if we fix our attention sharply enough to act spasmodically upon the muscles, even though we try to exert the will to prevent its moving. If a person in whose hands it works well will cross a field ten times, it will not turn in the same place at different times, especially if he vary his gait. This shows that it is in the man, and not in the "springs" of water.

Table-tipping, turning, etc., is the same thing. It results from the belief and attention of those taking part in it, operating spasmodically, but unconsciously, to them, through the muscles. We have not space, neither is it our purpose, to detail the experiment by which this can be clearly shown. The writing of *planchette* is due to the same phase of belief or expectancy, assisted by intense attention and sight. If the operator be blindfolded, the instrument will not work.

We may admit that all these vicious phases of life and action, — credulity, superstition, fanaticism, and expectant attention, — are species of belief, and gain by the admission. They may even have their attractions and yet not be dangerous, if we teach what they really are in their tendency.

There are serpents that are beautifully, exquisitely colored, and yet the moment that we see one to be a serpent it has no attractiveness. So we must show the demoralizing tendency of credulity, the enervating character of superstition, the recklessness of fanaticism, the serpentine nature of those "marvellous" performances through expectant attention, which is credulity gone mad, with method in its madness.

There are, however, distinctive beneficial phases of belief which are the source of comfort, inspiration, peace, and joy. We mention some of these.

Belief, we repeat, is prompt assent to, or acceptance of, that which we do not know with absolute certainty.

Expectancy is anticipation of future good, with sufficient reason for such an attitude of the mind. In belief there is necessarily no element of futurity. It has no regard to consequences. Belief simply takes what is absolutely known and applies such principles as are reliable, and then accepts as true that which known facts under these fixed principles indicate. When we add a new element we advance a step and give a relish to our belief, and it becomes expectancy.

There is little liability that men of intelligence and caution will err much in their belief, but in their expectations the danger increases. Our wishes are liable to modify our expectation. We shall gain something in the clearness of this mental condition if we test it carefully.

Reliance is the confident resting of the mind

upon such expectancy, satisfied, intellectually and emotionally, that it will bring us, through our active co-operation, that which we need. Expectancy makes us confident of the future; reliance links the present to the future and gives contentment now. This is akin to that which is spoken of as trust, but that word has such varied significance that it may as well be ignored in a series of definitions like these.

Faith, Christian faith, is belief developed into expectancy and reliance through affectionate, personal affiliation with Christ.

> "Faith builds a bridge across the gulf of death,
> To break the shock blind nature cannot shun,
> And lands thought smoothly on the farther shore."
> — YOUNG.

"That Christ may dwell in your hearts by faith."

"Faith is the substance of things hoped for, the evidence of things not seen."

"For by grace ye are saved through faith; and that not of yourselves: it is the gift of God."

Hope, Christian hope, is confident anticipation of that which, in our best frame of mind, we most desire. It is expectancy at its height. It is its choicest, best distilled possibilities.

> "The most vital movement mortals feel,
> Is hope, the balm and life-blood of the soul."

"Hope springs exultant on triumphant wing."

"Which hope we have as an anchor of the soul, both sure and steadfast, and which entereth into that within the vail."
— Heb. 6: 19.

Peace, Christian peace, is tranquil repose through faith and hope, regardless of the disturbances which would otherwise annoy. Ruskin says people are always expecting to get peace in Heaven, but that whatever peace they get there will be ready-made; that whatever of peace they can be blessed for must be on earth here. Life is scarcely worth the living that is not blessed with the power and privilege of peace, and it can only come as a fruit of belief.

"The fruit of righteousness is sown in peace of them that make peace."

"Thou wilt keep him in perfect peace whose mind is stayed on thee." — Is. 26: 3.

"The peace of God, which passeth all understanding, shall keep your hearts and minds through Christ Jesus." — Phil. 4: 7.

Joy, Christian joy, is the culmination of all the beneficent effects of belief in emotional exhilaration.

"Be glad in the Lord, and rejoice, ye righteous: and shout for joy, all ye that are upright in heart." — Ps. 32: 11.

"Rejoice in the Lord always; and again I say, Rejoice."
Phil. 3: 1.

Psychologists differ in their assignment of a home for belief. Some make it a child of the intellect, others of the emotions, and still others of the will. Each advocate makes so good a case for his theory that we incline to compound them, and make it an intellectual, emotional, and volitional activity. In no other way do we get a well-balanced view of it. Those who accept either limited view soon find themselves in difficulty. An intellectual belief, merely, is artistic, logical, serene, but is not fervent, touches no one, affects nothing in action. An emotional belief, merely, is æsthetic, fervid, ardent, but it is not logical, is not anchored in reason. It is more an instinct than a judgment. A volitional belief is ethical and determines results, it regulates the conduct by the principles of right and wrong. But it has no foundation judgment for its actions. It may not satisfy the theorists so well, but there is admirable psychological authority for defining and classifying belief as we have done, making it intelligent, emotional, and volitional.

Reasoning necessitates belief as one of its elements. In inductive reasoning, which passes from particulars to a general truth, belief plays an active part. We know the particulars, we believe the general truth. For instance, we know that every unsupported thing that we have seen falls to the ground, and we draw the general conclusion or form the belief that the earth attracts all bodies to itself. We afterwards observe that balloons do not fall, and our belief is disturbed by doubt. But if we study these exceptions that have caused us to doubt, we learn that it is the earth's attraction for the weightier air that has forced the balloons upward, that they are supported by the unseen air, and then we are confident that there is a way to explain all apparent exceptions to the rule, and we give prompt assent to the conclusion, and our belief is intelligent and firm.

In deductive reasoning which establishes a particular truth from a general, belief plays an indispensable part. For instance, —

No Christian steals,

This man steals,

Therefore this man is not a Christian.

The first requisite is belief in the first proposition. Without belief we cannot reason.

There are also different degrees and qualities of belief. Historical belief, requiring confidence in the reliability and disinterestedness of the chronicler, differs from scientific belief that rests upon confidence in the facilities, faithfulness, and ability of an advocate, or upon the thoroughness and reliability of our own investigations. Personal belief in the integrity and honor of a friend involves confidence in our opportunities to know, and discernment in estimating his strength and weakness; which is quite distinct from religious belief, which necessitates devout allegiance to God because of His supremacy and beneficence, together with affectionate reliance upon and confidence in Him.

Clear discriminations in this direction will incline the young to estimate the appeals made to them, reducing the liability of being swept into credulity on the one side and disbelief on the other.

Childhood is the age of credulity, and the temptation is great to intensify this tendency. There is never harm in the native play of credulity more than in the frolic of a colt, but to develop it into superstition is as sinful as it is cruel. To check credulity in early life is liable to wreck the native tendency to belief forever There is a golden mean to be sought, and while youth are still buoyant with hope, they are to be taught and practised in restraint, and given the proper stimulus of faith.

Youth above fifteen,— *i. e.*, when they first experience the stern realities of life — become doubters, unbelievers, very easily, and need to be promptly, wisely, fervently directed in right ways.

As the courts demand that a man who has hitherto borne a good reputation shall be considered innocent until he be proved guilty, so belief is not to be scandalized by doubt until special definite experience arrests it and is able at least to present an indictment against it.

The position which some assume, that doubt is an inherent virtue, needs to be thoroughly ventilated, and its innate viciousness exposed. Intelligent belief is a virtue, is restful and satisfying; it conserves all mental and moral forces, it places the faculties in readiness for action. Doubt, so far as it leans to disbelief, is a misfortune, is a physical, mental, and moral disturbance, is unsatisfying, wastes energy, and unnerves for all good work.

> "Our doubts are traitors,
> And make us lose the good we oft might win,
> By fearing to attempt."

No youth should go from the Sunday-school without knowing that experience will challenge his belief, but that for him to be on the alert for opportunities to doubt is to make himself in his own mental life what the scandal-monger is in society.

Our own unflinching, intelligent loyalty to the truth we teach is pre-eminently important. A judicial habit of mind in weighing and estimating facts is essential to success in forming our own belief, and in moulding the belief of others.

Verbal expression intensifies belief. A clear statement of a truth is of itself mental and emotional power. No brilliancy of intellectual effort is so effective, no fervency of emotion is more effective, than a clear, verbal expression of a belief. Doubt yields to no human attack more readily than to an explicit, luminous statement of a belief. Words well arranged in definition are like an army drawn up in battle array. The

Bible demand for verbal confession of our faith is strictly philosophical in its bearing upon life, thought, and emotion. "With the heart man believeth unto righteousness; and *with the mouth confession is made unto salvation*" (Rom. 10 : 10).

Thus grouping the Scripture truths, we may teach the philosophy of Divine truth; the æsthetics of Christianity, or how to balance the emotional life so that it shall be aglow with sacred fervor without being weak and nerveless; the ethics of Christianity, or how to choose the right with fearless steadfastness, without fanaticism.

Belief is not matured until it embodies itself in action. It is the weakest sentimentality that talks of believing what is not lived up to. Acts performed for the mere pleasure they bring do not indicate belief. Acts done with deliberate disregard of present consequences, for the sake of principle and its future reward, indicate belief. Readiness to act should an opportunity present itself signifies as much as defined action under other conditions.

The materialization of belief in action, the

crystallization of thought in deed, is indispensable. It is a philosophic tribute to the wisdom of the apostolic assurance that faith without works is dead.

> "If faith produce no works, I see,
> That faith is not a living tree.
> Thus faith and works together grow:
> No separate life they e'er can know:
> They're soul and body, hand and heart;
> What God hath joined, let no man part."

The motive of belief or disbelief can be can canvassed with profit. An agent who presents a book, machine, or mine has a different motive from the neighbor who asks you to join him in sending a Thanksgiving turkey to a family whom adverse circumstances have clouded; the politician appeals to you from a different motive from the statesman; the fanatical, self-conscious reformer has a different motive from the quiet, undemonstrative lover of mankind who seeks the greatest good of the greatest number with the least social or political upheaval; a credulous specialist in religion, who urges belief in some eccentricity of faith, has a different motive from him who invites allegiance to the truth of God in its spirit and power; the skeptic, who attempts to win you to disbelief, differs in motive from the man who seeks to bring you into a state of loyalty to a personal Saviour, who calls for affectionate sacrifice.

To be skilled in estimating the motives of those who would secure our belief or disbelief, tends to balance our emotions, and always leads to greater confidence in those who, from disinterested motives, appeal for belief in the eternal verities.

The bodily and mental condition is responsible for a quickened tendency through transitory emotions to doubt, disbelief, despondency, and despair, and this needs to be so definitely and clearly understood in advance that when these physically engendered experiences come they will have been robbed of their power to attach themselves as habits of mind, prompting us, instead of brooding over them, to devote ourselves to reinvigorating the system to prevent their continuance or reappearance. This is a very important consideration. Many excellent Christians lose much enjoyment from mistaken ideas on this point.

The work of the Sunday-school is to teach belief in God and His Word. We are to teach belief in the existence of God. The child, in all probability, believes this, but there is a liability to his having this belief shaken by the ruthless assaults of skeptically vicious men. It is therefore important that children know what reason there is for their belief, aside from the fact that they do believe. It is not necessary that we elaborate the logical argument for the existence of God, but we may wisely call attention to what we know of the works of God in nature, which indicate a supreme mind as conceiving the idea of this universe in all its parts and varieties. It is a never-failing source of interest, as well as profit, to dwell upon the adaptability of every created object to other creations. Before aught was created, the whole must have been conceived. It is well to follow this by calling attention to what we know of nature as indicating the command of force in creation, or in realizing that which had been planned. It is easy to entertain and delight children with the skill required to make anything with tools, and show them how much intellect and patience it takes to do well any mechanical work of high order. Thus, from what they know it is easy to establish a belief, or, rather, give a reason for the belief they already have. In the same line may be shown the tendency of all force to exhaust itself when applied, or the impossibility of perpetual motion, and yet the power behind all created objects and forces is inexhaustible. Thus we may explain belief in God as the Preserver of the universe, as the everliving and ever-present, the all-knowing and all-powerful Father and Author of all things. In the same way we may explain our belief in God from what we know of Him as reflected in our own nature.

We need so to teach belief in the existence of God that all tendencies and temptations to doubt shall be harmless; that youth may escape the horrors of disbelief, which brings in its wake despair and desperation: that they may avoid the evils of credulity, superstition, and fanaticism; that they shall have an intelligent faith, an affectionate reliance, a devout love, a profound peace, a serene hope, and an exhilarating joy.

An intelligent belief in the Scriptures is indispensable; and this requires a judicious use of what is known in substantiating what is believed.

One line of facts or class of knowledge may be stated thus. Man is capable of performing voluntary acts in which he is more or less influenced by the supposed approval or disapproval of a Supreme Power. Man clearly believes in such a power, and acts with a distinct impression that that Being has a law which we keep or violate in all moral action.

If there be a Supreme Being, if He rules, if He has a law, and that law is not revealed, how can there be accountability? All admit that it is revealed in natural indications; the Christian thinks that natural revelation is insufficient to establish moral character. Is there anything therein relating to temperance, patience, godliness, brotherly love, charity, worship, prayer, forgiveness, a future state, etc.?

With human reason unreliable, undisciplined, biased, what could be the authority for interpreting nature into a code of moral laws, even if they were foreshadowed there? Is n't it a well-nigh universal law that, even with the explicit Word of God, men incline to establish rules according to their practice, instead of practising according to the rules of God's word.

From nature we do not get all the laws we need, and no authority for those we do get. The truths we find in nature now, we should not have found but for their revelation in Scripture.

The Scriptures teach all that man needs to know of God; of Divine providence; of duty to self, to fellow men, and to God; of the future state, of salvation, worship, prayer, peace, hope, and joy.

We know our need; we know our inability to supply that need in any other way; we know the Bible fully meets every moral need of man,— hence we are justified in believing the Scriptures to be the law of God concerning man's duties.

Another line of facts may be stated thus: It is clearly demonstrable that most of the books of the Bible were written by the persons who claim their authorship; that the books were written when they claim to have been; that they are substantially the same as when written; that the writers were men who deserve the confidence of all ages; that all the doctrines are beneficial; that the moral tendency is higher than that found in any other philosophy; that the Scriptures have a marvellous power of diffusing their truth through all nationalities — no barbarous nation being unsusceptible to their civilizing, moralizing influence; that they have actually made the civilized nations of earth what they are for good; that they have uniformly made man purer, more upright, more charitable, more holy.

We know all this, and are justified, because of this knowledge, in believing the Scriptures to be the Word of God to man.

In this way we might call attention to what we know as the foundation of our belief in the omnipotence, omnipresence, omniscience, immutability, goodness, and holiness of God; in the divinity of Christ; in the humanity of Christ; in the personality of the Holy Ghost; in the sinful state of man; in the principles of redemption; in the duties of submission, love, and trust in God; in the duty to pray and praise; in the duty to observe the Sabbath; in the duties of charity, justice, and love for our fellow men; in the divine appointment of the church and its sacred ordinances and sacraments.

There is temptation to pause on each of these interesting themes and call attention to what we know, and the way in which our knowledge culminates in belief. But our aim does not warrant it. We have done all that was contemplated if we have emphasized with sufficient clearness the importance of training the youth to know when they believe how and why they believe so that their belief will not be shaken when they meet the experiences of life. We hope it may aid to an intelligent, steadfast acknowledgment of allegiance to the Divine Master, and affectionate reliance upon a personal Saviour.

ART OF CHOOSING.

> " Decide not rashly. The decision made,
> Can never be recalled. The Gods implore not
> Plead not, solicit not: they only offer
> Choice and occasion, which, once being passed,
> Return no more." — LONGFELLOW.

" Once to every man and nation comes the moment to decide,
In the strife of Truth with Falsehood, for the good or evil side."
— LOWELL.

" Choose you this day whom ye will serve." — JOSH. 24 : 15.

" The strongest principle of growth lies in human choice."
— GEORGE ELIOT.

" Choose always the way that seems the best, however rough it may be. Custom will render it easy and agreeable." — PYTHAGORAS.

" Men must be decided in what they will not do, and then they are able to act with vigor in what they ought to do." — MENCEIRS.

CHAPTER X.

ART OF CHOOSING.

AN explicit choice, with all that it involves, is one of the highest acts of the human mind. Choice is the selection of one of two or more lines of thought or activity. It is not necessarily voluntary. The will is deliberately ignored in a large number of our selections of a mode of activity.

The choice may be impulsive, unguided, unconscious, and purposeless. The child's first manifestations of activity and power are of this character. There is a possibility of this random selection's continuing through life. It leads to thriftlessness in business, laxity in morals, inconstancy in religion.

In the next higher phase, choice is formed by, or responds to, external stimulation. It is the result of circumstances and not of conscious purpose. Circumstances inevitably affect all minds. They have their legitimate place, and should be duly considered in making choice. There is no excuse, however, in being their servant, much less their slave. Those who have not risen above this plane are weak and vacillating. There is nothing reliable in their anticipations. They have neither a harbor in which to anchor, nor a chart by which to sail. It is an advance on the spontaneous, random activity, because it has the rudiments of allegiance, with more or less indication of permanency.

In a still higher phase, choice is based on the imitative tendency of the human mind to act without perceptible motive, and simply because others do the same thing in the same way. Fashions prove its social tyranny. Many of the social vicious habits are at first largely a matter of imitation. While good sometimes comes therefrom, it is a dangerous as well as a weak attitude for the human mind to assume in making choice.

In these three methods of choice,— at random, from circumstances, by imitation, the will is neglected, ignored. Much of the intemperance, licentiousness, shiftlessness, thriftlessness, poverty, and disease of the world comes from making no use of the will. There may be a species of goodness without it, but there is no high type of manhood or womanhood that does not utilize the will, that does not enthrone it.

The mind, from an early age, is active, and usually acts in one of these unreliable ways through life, unless trained by experience or instruction to more perfect action through the will.

The will increases in power and skill by exercise, and it is to little purpose that we appeal to its higher possibilities, until it has been educated by discipline. Exercise in these lower ranges of activity tends to develop higher conditions. There is a weak and vicious sentimentality that would leave the child's habit of religious thought alone until he is of age to make the supreme choice intelligently.

It is philosophic art to direct the spontaneous, purposeless mental activity into the best channels by every legitimate external influence and imitative inclination available. Then, when he reaches an age or comes into circumstances where conscious choice is probable, he will have established habits of activity that incline him to the right.

We have thus far considered the three methods of choice that are practically involuntary. There is no strength of mind, no moral safety, so long as there is lacking voluntary power, or direct volitional choice. The will must be enthroned. It must consciously direct the various powers of the mind. Until it thus exercises supremacy there is no balance, no safety.

The will is the servant of the intellect, in that, at its best estate, it takes its authority from reason and judgment. It is the associate of the intellect, in that it consults with it in the act of deliberation which always precedes a proper choice. It is the master ruler of the intellect in that, when it has done its work as servant faithfully, as associate companionably, it is duly enthroned, and allowed to direct and dictate the object, method, and intensity of thought.

Similarly it is the servant, companion, and master of the emotional nature. The quality and quantity of manhood depend largely upon which of these relations the will sustains to the intellect and the emotions.

But beyond that there is no assurance of permanency so long as the will has to be always on the alert. It must reach a condition in which it makes right choice without conscious exertion.

The art of conserving will power is to train the volitional phase of our nature to do its work to the best advantage with the least consciousness of effort. To gain this end, it is necessary, when the will assumes the mastery over thought, feeling, and action, that it do its work methodically.

It must acquire the skill to *deliberate*, or weigh motives, arguments, and appeals, to select different lines of activity, only one of which can be adopted. The art of deliberating is most important. The consideration and meditation which it implies is vital to reliability in choice.

> "Deliberate with thyself:
> Pause, ponder, sift; not eager in the choice,
> Nor jealous of the chosen: fixing, fix;
> Judge before friendship, then confide till death."
> — YOUNG.

There are times in which no deliberation is

needed, when, in short, it is almost a crime to hesitate. There are occasions when he who hesitates is lost. It is a safe rule to follow, that if we incline to do a thing and don't know whether we ought, then do it not; if we incline not to do a thing, but think perhaps we ought, then do it.

To decide is to cut off deliberation. We gain much by having that decision of character which leads us to know when not to deliberate, when to cease deliberation. Some principles of action are vital in this matter.

We must avoid all rash decisions, all decisions under prejudice, in temper, from jealousy or envy. When the mind is not in proper balance we must not consent to make a decision.

> "The decision made
> Can never be recalled. The gods implore not,
> Plead not, solicit not; they only offer
> Choice and occasion, which once being past
> Return no more."
> — LONGFELLOW.

The way in which we make our decisions is specially important, indicating the breadth and depth of our mental powers. There is a weak and almost criminal way of allowing our decisions to be formed by the influence of signs. Persons of immature will power, who have never associated as they should the intellect with the will, frequently acquire a habit of making most of their choices dependent upon some relic of barbarism that tradition has handed down the generations.

The grandmother telling fortunes with the tea-grounds did an injury to the young minds that she little suspected. The nursery-maid who is allowed to discipline the children by means of signs leaves a permanent impress of evil with the child.

Impressions are frequently allowed to tyrannize through the decisions. People frequently train themselves to consult their impressions before they decide. Others make most of their decisions from their prejudices. Prejudice is an obstacle to all sincerity and wisdom in the matter of choice. In proportion to the strength of our prejudices is our mental weakness to be largely estimated. As we value our reputation for candor and good judgment must we escape the danger of deciding from prejudice.

Decision, in its best estate, is prompt, energetic, and unbiassed. It is influenced by the highest considerations of duty.

"Once to every man and nation comes the moment to decide,
In the strife of Truth with Falsehood, for the good or evil
side." — LOWELL.

Determination, or absolute direction to a certain end, is decision fixed, established so that it will, under ordinary circumstances, adhere to its purpose. Many who, in revival excitement, decide to be on the Lord's side, and from impulse, from circumstance, or from imitative tendency, choose Christ as their friend, soon relapse into an indifferent state, not because they were insincere, but because their decision did not eventuate in determination.

Emerson said that he only was a well-made man who had a good determination.

Decision affects us in one matter, makes one choice, while determination settles causes of action, establishes, in the nature of the case, principles of choice that determine what future choices shall be. It takes our decisions out of the realm of chance and fickleness.

Our determination, like everything else in mental life, needs its own principles of action.

The greater the number of judicious laws it can establish for its own guidance, the better. It wants to settle upon as many classes of things that it will not do under any circumstances, as possible. This removes the necessity of any decision in that class of cases. There is no temptation when we have fixed upon certain things that will, under no condition, be done. In the same way we need to settle upon those classes of things that we will do without meditation or consideration. In short, the secret of success in this direction is in reducing to the minimum the number of cases in which we shall deliberate.

This latter phase of determination shades off into *resolution*, which shuts off the possibility of further consideration. It indicates a settled purpose to decide as we have resolved, regardless of consequences.

When Paul started for Jerusalem and stopped a few days with the disciples at Tyre, and the Tyrians did everything in their power to dissuade him from pursuing his way, he was deaf to all their entreaties, because of his high resolve. Later, he stoped at Cæsarea, where one Agabus of Judea, with dramatic effect, took Paul's girdle and bound his own hands and feet, and said, "Thus saith the Holy Ghost, So shall the Jews at Jerusalem bind the man that owneth this girdle, and shall deliver him into the hands of the Gentiles." But these things had no effect in changing his purpose, for he had resolved, after due deliberation, what to do, and nothing thereafter moved him.

Resolution always gives courage. To know what not to do and what to do settles many things, the uncertainty of which makes us cowards. We rarely falter in any emergency, rarely fear anything when we are sure we are right and are resolved to conquer. Let two men face the same adventure, the one knowing in advance that he wants to do it, and is resolved, if possible, upon it, and the other undecided whether he wants to do it or not; and it does not take long to know which will be successful.

Longfellow says, in the *Masque of Pandora*, "Resolve, and thou art free." This is true only when resolve has its higher, fuller meaning, when it is more than mere decision.

Goethe says, "He who is firm in will moulds

the world to himself." There is in this a universal truth. By will is here meant that resolution which comes from determined, perpetual decision, resulting from due deliberation when the emotional nature acquiesces.

The involuntary choices are those decisions that are spontaneous or random; that eventuate from circumstances or external influence; that follow the imitative tendency.

The voluntary choices are those decisions that result from deliberation. But there is no safety so long as the will is required to keep its grip on the choice. The power of voluntary choice lies in that maturity of the habit of deciding on the lines of principles that we have well established, which makes it certain in advance how we shall decide, so that when we face any emergency that special decision is made in advance. Thus our voluntary choices become involuntary, not in the former sense, but in the sense that no immediate act of the will is required, but we take advantage of previous and more deliberate choice of principles of decision and action.

Naturalists group all living things into species,

genera, families, orders, classes, kingdoms. Every weed and insect, every flower and bird, everything that grows, finds its place in some one of these species, of which there is an endless number, in some genus of which there are much fewer, in some family, order, or class, and the number in each ascending scale is much less. It does not require a fractional part of the time or thought to tell in what class a thing is, that it does to tell its species. And all the infinite array of species are in one of the two kingdoms, animal or vegetable, and the most illiterate place objects in their proper kingdom without expenditure of brain power.

Theoretically, we might expect scientists to begin with the species and then work up the scale to the kingdom, but that would be a practical impossibility. There is no feasible, no scientific way but to begin at the top, deciding upon the kingdom, class, order, family, genus, and species in due procession.

There is no other scientific way of making choices in the moral, intellectual, or religious life. Those moralists who would have us make each decision by itself, placing each choice in some species, require a practical impossibility.

Our choices are in reality grouped like kingdoms into classes, orders, families, genera, and species, and, like the scientist, we must begin at the top and run down the scale.

The primal choice of every soul is between allegiance to God or disloyalty to Him.

There are but two kingdoms in choice, — the kingdom of Heaven, or permanent absence from it. Every choice is for one of these two kingdoms.

Establish this resolution, firm and inflexible, let every decision be made without deliberation or meditation, that we will do nothing that can by any possibility lessen our chance of gaining the Heavenly kingdom, and that we will do everything that can by any possibility improve our reward in it, and then we have settled the vast multitude of questions that would else perplex us. Every question that vexes us grows out of a willingness to do all the doubtful things we can, and still claim allegiance, and leave undone all the duties we can, and still hope for a place in the Heavenly kingdom. Whoever takes the higher plane of choice has all these problems solved for him.

Beyond that, however, there are minor decisions as to means to be used, methods to be adopted, etc., but it is not our purpose to pursue this thought further than to show that we want that choice of Christ which shall forever establish the resolution through deliberation and decision, by which we shall invariably, without conscious effort of the will, choose only those courses of action, means and methods of activity, which shall in the highest sense promote the glory of God.

The motives actuating choice are numerous, but they mostly come from desire in some form. While the character is the combination of all the qualities of mind and heart, it may be said to depend largely, if not entirely, upon the quality and strength of longing for experiences or gratifications. The nature, direction, intensity, and balance of these longings indicate the motive behind, and the power directing our actions.

> "Our deeds have travelled with us from afar,
> And what we have been makes us what we are."

Behind every deed there has been a longing gratified, suppressed, or denied.

A wish is a strong inclination to have something that is not near at hand, and may or may not be accessible.

A desire is imperious, commanding, and is centred upon something attainable at once.

To covet is to desire that which another has, or which we can only get through another. Covetousness is a dangerous motive to reign over our decisions, and yet it is one to which all youth are liable.

Almost everything looks better when another applies it than when viewed in the abstract; as a garment is more attractive when worn by a stylish, graceful person than it is in the store with a hundred others. Oratory in the abstract attracts few, but multitudes covet the art as they listen to the eloquence of a living, electrifying orator. Multitudes of people have few wishes or desires that are not born of what they see in others.

Our choice is not, cannot be, wise and best until we are educated above covetousness. We must suppress it, or supplant it with higher wishes and desires. Its evils are many, not the least of which is that we lose what we have in seeking what others have; we fail to be what we might be by trying in vain to be what another is.

Desires need to be moderated, toned down, put into the traces, while our wishes need to be limited, more defined, more tangible. Our desires contract, our wishes scatter.

We shall find the Word of God the most effective instrumentality in all the range of forces with which to suppress covetousness, moderate desire, and limit wishes. No other book presents such motives, or furnishes such material from which to modulate its various phases.

We must educate the mind to be influenced by results that are remote in point of time and distance. Neglect of this leads to all the physical, social, financial vices of the world. If we allow children to choose those pleasures that gratify the surface senses, that yield the quickest emotional delight, that bring the most speedy reward, we may as well understand that base appetites will be formed and gratified, social vices yielded to, dishonesty and kindred financial vagaries employed, if temptations present themselves.

There is no way possible to train the young to a proper appreciation of the value of more remote rewards and dangers except through the Bible.

The idea of God in his omniscience, of eternity in its scope, of holiness in its ideality, of Christ in his sacrifice, all make the present seem small and unimportant in comparison with these vast interests.

The Commandments, the Sermon on the Mount, the Lord's Prayer, the Parables, the Psalms, the Prophecies, Epistles, all prompt man to take a long range of vision. It is a great benefit to near-sighted people to live on a prairie, where their view is always limitless.

The range of moral vision is extended by much meditation upon God, and earnest, persistent study of His works and Word.

This phase of desire is personal. There is a higher view to take in making choice of activity, namely, the need others have of our service, the good that will come to others from our choice. There is a responsibility involved in our relation to others as germinant in our choice, that we cannot afford to forget or neglect.

The world is threatened by no one phase of social life, more than by that which represents every man, party, and interest as looking after its own affairs. Politics, mercantile life, social life are all seriously jeopardized by the too general tendency to make our choice dependent upon some good that will eventually come to us. Scientists, philosophers, philanthropists have nothing to offer by way of improving this state of things.

The remedy is in God's Word. Its tone from beginning to end emphasizes the value to man of making his choice with a view to its effect upon others. Our relation to God, to Christ, to each other, make it at once a privilege and a duty to consider others in estimating the importance of each choice. The idea so often taught, that we are members one of another, that we ought to bear one another's burdens; the conception of Christian brotherhood; the injunction to love one another; the reminder to forgive as we hope to be forgiven, by the very atmosphere they produce inspire us to choose in every event in life with reference to the effect our activity, based on that choice, will have on others.

There is a higher plane than any of these upon which we may live, and that is one in which all our choices come from a desire to obey and please a personal God, whom we fear too much not to obey, whom we reverence too much not to seek to please, whom we appreciate too keenly to neglect, whom we love too tenderly to slight in our estimates of motives. The Bible, in its entire tone and tenor, serves to bring us into this relation to our Father, Saviour, and Comforter.

The motive to choice, must centre in God, and in our personal, affectionate relation to him.

Another element of choice that is not to be overlooked, is the fact that it is the embodiment of much in little. It is the concentration of all emotions and motives of activity, for a long time to come, in one effort of the will. It represents infinitely more than it is. As the Claude Loraine glass brings a vast landscape in perfect proportion and clear outline into one small frame, so choice gathers extended consequences into one simple act. Only as this is appreciated, and as each decision is made with reference to the chain of consequences that naturally follow, is there wisdom in choice.

Special divine enlightenment may come to man, — in a mild sense does frequently come, — making his decisions more significant. The mind, through the higher emotional instincts, may be brought to concentrate knowledge of personal need, eventual reward, responsibility to man, duty and affection to God, with such clearness and inspiration as to leave no doubt, no vein of hesitancy. There may be a peculiarly vivid sense of past wrong-doing and present sinfulness. All these mental attitudes into which it is possible to be brought by some special experience are more or less approximated in conversion.

Perhaps no one instance has been more marked or more generally known than that of the conversion of Henry F. Durant, Esq. Ex-Governor Gaston, of Boston, in what will probably stand as the grandest jury argument of his life, made this most remarkable allusion to Mr. Durant's conversion. After referring to his almost matchless legal ability, he said, in substance: "I have not the ability to appreciate the experience of Henry F. Durant, but this we all know, that about the time his only child died, he had a religious experience, so deep, so profound, so impressive, that he never after practised the profession to which he had hitherto given his life, in which he had taken unbounded pleasure, and won high fame. From the day of that experience, Mr. and Mrs. Durant devoted their time, their thought, their energy, their wealth, to religious, charitable, and educational advancement."

This illustrates the possibilities there are of swaying the entire life out of long-established intellectual, emotional, and deliberately selected ways into entirely distinct and different channels, under special divine guidance, through the conscience and the emotions.

Choice at such a moment, under such inspirations, is not unnatural, is not supernatural, but is the embodiment of all the highest human possibilities of thought, emotion, and will, stimulated, enlightened, and empowered by a personal God, who seems to touch the human soul through direct affiliation. This it is that man may experience — that multitudes have experienced — in conversion. This choice, supreme, permanent, intense, exalts every human attribute, and through the Holy Spirit clothes it with a power and eternity of purpose never known before.

The soul that has not made such choice has missed the grandest experience of life.

INDEX.

Abraham, 33.
Adaptation of life to truth, 27.
    of text to age, 23.
Addison, quotation, 18.
Age, analytical, 22, 30.
    inquisitive, 29.
    memory, 23.
    under seven or eight, 29.
    between seven and fifteen, 29.
    above fifteen, 29, 30.
Aim of Sunday-school, 21.
Amusements, 148, 150.
Application of truth, 26.
    falsely made, 60.
Appreciation of single truths, 48.
    of steps in process, 50.
Art of Choosing, 201.
    of Remembering, 91.
    of Thinking, 45.
Art Club of Boston, 52.
Associative aids, 28.
Attention, 75.
    abstract, 78.
    adaptation to age, 84.
    application to Bible study, 79.
    automatic, 85.
    change of, 111.
    difficulty of, 75.
    expectant, 177.
    external, 77.
    internal, 77.
    involuntary, 75, 85.
    voluntary, 85.
Authority, parental, 32.
Awakening interest, 102.

Bad habits, 110.
Bailey, quotation, 162.
Bain, quotation, 130.
Ball-room, sympathy, 149.
Beaver, an illustration, 78.
Bee, an illustration, 21.
Belief, 167, 181.
    adaptation of, 186.
    certainty of, 164.
    commercial, 166.
    credulity in, 175.
    fanaticism in, 176.
    foundation facts of, 166.
    motives, 190.
    scientific, 166.
    social, 166.
    responsibilities of, 191.
Benefit of sympathy, 145.
Bible, how taught, 14.
    in olden days, 15.
    text-book, 13.
    underlying principles, 14.
    what it does for mankind, 13.
Biography, 29.
Broken-hearted parents, 121.
Byron, a quotation, 44.
Business men as thinkers, 45.

Carlyle, a quotation, 144.
Carpenter, Dr. W. B., authority, 178.
Certainty in belief, 169.
Change of attention, 111.
Character development, 22.
Chemists' art, 56.
Child and mother, 112.
Children, relation of parents, 37.
    relation to parents, 36.
Choice, circumstantial, 201.
    deliberative, 205.

Choice, decisive, 206.
   generous, 218.
   imitative, 202.
   impulsive, 201.
   involuntary, 201.
   selfish, 218.
   voluntary, 204.
Choosing, Art of, 201.
Christian living, requirements, 21.
   science, 132.
Churchill, a quotation, 144.
Church service, 151.
Circumstances and associations, 28.
Classification of age, 31.
Claude Loraine glass, 219.
Cobbe, Frances Power, quotation, 173.
Coleridge, S. T., illustration, 80.
Comparison of truth, 55.
Comprehension of responsibilities, 20.
Conditions of success, 123.
Confession, 188.
Contemporary review, quotation, 173.
Covetousness, 215.
Cranch, quotation, 44.
Credulity, 175.
Criticism, effects of, 14.
   not intended, 16.
Critics, 55.
Currie, quotation, 74.
Cyclamen, illustration, 30.

Decision, 206.
Deductive reasoning, 63.
Definition, 51.
Deformities, righting physical, 107
Deliberation, 205.
Denham, quotation, 162.
Desire, 215.
Despair, 171.
Desperation, 172.
Despondency, 171.
Determination, 208.
Development of mind, 20
Disbelief, 170.
Discriminate to note differences, 51
   what is to be remembered, 102
Divine guidance, 219.
   will, 21.

Dorr, Julia C. R., quotation, 18.
Doubt, 168.
Drunkards, reformed, 111.
Durant, H. F., 220.

Eagle, an illustration, 78.
Effect of imagination, 122.
Eliot, George, quotation, 144.
Elocution teacher, an illustration, 131.
Emerson, quotations, 18, 162.
Emotions, defined, 131.
   developed, 137.
   excessive, 135.
   influence of, 132.
   influence of word of God upon, 140.
   lack of self-control, 133.
   painful, 134.
   pleasurable, 134.
Emotional sympathy, 147.
Emphasis in Bible reading, 54.
Enemies, relation to, 39.
Erratic Christians, 127.
   emotional natures, 135.
Estimating consequences, 57.
Examples of deductive reasoning, 70.
Excessive emotional natures, 135.
Expectancy, 181.
Expectant attention, 177.
External attention, 77.

Faculty born with us, 18.
Faith, 182.
Faith and works, 189.
Fanaticism, 176.
Feelings, muscular, 131.
   sensations, 131.
Fish, an illustration, 100.
Forgetfulness, 93.
Fortunes without paying debts, 57.
Foundation of good thinking, 49.
Fragrant flowers an illustration, 35
Friends, 38.
Froude, quotation, 162.
Fuller, quotation, 90.

Gaston, ex-Governor, 220.
Geography, 28.
Glorious old days, 15.

INDEX.   225

Goethe, quotation, 211.
Grouping texts, 30.

Habits, bad, 107.
    conditions of, 108.
    creates brain power, 109.
    good, 107.
    in early rising, 109.
    in morality, 114.
    in religion, 115.
    Philosophy of, 107.
    relieves the will, 108.
    use of, 108.
Habitual indifference, 113.
Hamilton, Sir William, 79.
Hare, quotation, 144.
Harmony is power, 146.
Havergal, quotation, 162.
Hazel fork, 179.
Hemans, Mrs., quotation, 144.
History of Bible, how taught, 28.
Hope, 182.
Humming-bird, an illustration, 80.

Ice-cutting, an illustration, 109.
Illustrations:
    Beaver, 78.
    Bee, 21.
    Coleridge, S. T., 80.
    Cyclamen, 30.
    Drawing line, 19.
    Eagle, 78.
    Elocution teacher, 131.
    Fish, 35.
    Fragrant flowers, 35.
    Humming-bird, 80.
    Ice-cutting, 109.
    Jasper, Rev. John, 46.
    Leafing of tree, 137.
    Mozart, 147.
    Musical development, 41.
    Musicians, trained, 134.
    Oats on cotton, 59.
    Satchel, 95.
    Silkworm, 27.
    Spider eats double, 58.
    Spider's web, 97.
    Soldiers in step, 145.
    Starting tuns, 19.
    Strawberry, 25.
    Telescope, 84.
    Tempering steel, 169.

Illustrations (continued).
    Weeds, 35.
Imagination, develops virtue, 121.
    development of, 124.
    influence of, 121.
    neglect of, 123.
    Use of, 121.
    well trained, 128.
Immature state of mind, 24.
Imitative choice, 20.
Importance of S. S. work, 13.
Impressions, 207.
Impulsive choice, 201.
Individual texts, 23.
Inductive reasoning, 61.
Influence of emotions, 132.
    of imagination, 121.
Ingersoll, 22.
Internal attention, 77.
Interesting Bible study, 102.
Inquisitive age, 29.
Intellectual sympathy, 146.
Intemperates reformed, 112.
International lessons, 14, 15.
Introduction, 13.
Involuntary attention, 75.
    choice, 201.
    recollection, 94.

Jasper, Rev. John, 46.
Joy, 183.
Juries, 149.

Landor, quotations, 44, 74, 90.
Laws of logic, 65.
Lawyers' power, 53.
Leafing of tree an illustration, 137
Leland, quotation, 162.
Life fashioned by truth, 27.
Lived religion away from home, 60
Longfellow, quotations, 18, 206, 210.
Lowell, quotation, 208.

Memory age, 23.
    a panorama, 90.
Memorizing a drudgery, 26.
Meredith, Owen, quotation, 44.
Mental development, defined, 20.
    principles of, 20.
    too early, 25.
Methods and principles, 17.

Moody, 22.
Morality, 114.
Mother's tact, 122.
Motives of choice, 214.
Mozart, an illustration, 147.
Musical development, an illustration, 41.
Music teaching, an illustration, 49.
Muscular feeling, 131.

Napoleon, quotation, 120.
Naturalists, 212.
Novalis, quotation, 130.

Oats on cotton, 59.
Outline for grouping, 34.

Painful emotions, 134.
Parents, relation to children, 36.
Parental authority, 32.
Patent Office, 57.
Paul and the Tyrians, 209.
Peace, 183.
Penmanship, teaching, 49.
Philosophy of Belief, 163.
    of Habit, 107,
    of Sympathy, 145.
Physical sympathy, 145.
Physician's success, 53.
Physicians, untrained, 57.
Planchette, 180.
Pleasant emotions, 133.
Psychology to be popularized, 14.
Principles of logic, 64.

Quotations:
    Addison, 18.
    Bailey, 162.
    Bain, 130.
    Byron, 44.
    Carlyle, 144.
    Churchill, 144.
    Cobbe, Frances Power, 173.
    Contemporary Review, 173.
    Cranch, 44.
    Currie, 74.
    Denham, 162.
    Dorr, Julia C. R., 18.
    Eliot, Geo., 144.
    Emerson, 18, 162.
    Froude, 162.
    Fuller, 90.

Quotations (*continued*).
    Gaston, Ex-Gov., 220.
    Goethe, 211.
    Hamilton, Sir William, 79.
    Hare, 144.
    Havergal, 162.
    Hemans, Mrs., 144.
    Landon, 44, 74, 90.
    Leland, 162.
    Longfellow, 18, 206, 210.
    Lowell, 208.
    Meredith, Owen, 44.
    Napoleon, 120.
    Novalis, 130.
    Rogers, 90.
    Scott, 130.
    Shakespeare, 90, 106.
    Shelley, 44.
    Sidney, 44.
    Spurgeon, 144.
    Webster, 106, 120.
    Young, 162, 182, 205.

Recreation, 151.
Relation to enemies, 39.
    to friends, 38.
    of parents to children, 37.
    to parents, 36.
Reliance, 181.
Religion, definition, 115.
Remembering, Art of, 91.
Resolution, 209.
Revision Committee, 25.
Rhythmical verses, 27.
Rogers, quotation, 90.
Ruskin's texts, 27.

Satchel, an illustration, 95.
Scholarly men recreant, 123.
Scott, quotation, 130.
Scripture References:
    Exodus, xv., xx., — 28.
    Leviticus, xix. 3, — 36.
    Deuteronomy, v. 16; xxvii. 16, — 36.
    vi. 7, 8, — 37.
    2 Samuel, i. 7, 27, — 28.
    1 Kings, viii., — 28.
    1 Chronicles, xxix. 18, — 120.
    Psalms, xxiii., xxxii., xc., xci., ciii., cxii., cxix., cxxxix., — 28.

Scripture References (*continued*).
  Psalms, cxxxvii. 6, — 90.
  Proverbs, ii., iii., viii., xii., — 28.
    xxiii. 22, — 36.
    vi. 20, 21 ; xxii. 6, — 37.
    xiii. 18, 24 ; xvii. 17 ; xviii. 24 ; xxii. 24 ; xxvii. 6, 19 ; xxix. 15, 17, — 38.
    xxi. 10, — 39.
    iv. 1, 20 ; vii. 24, — 74.
  Ecclesiastes, iv. 9, 10, — 38.
    xii. 1, — 90.
  Isaiah, lviii., — 28.
  Amos, iii. 3, — 38.
  Zachariah, vii. 10, — 120.
  Matthew, v., vi., vii., — 28.
    v. 23, 25, 44, — 39.
    vi. 12, — 39.
    xviii. 23-35, — 39.
    xxii. 42, — 44.
  Mark, xi. 25, 26, — 39.
  Luke, xviii. 18, 19, — 37.
  John, iv. 9-26 ; xxi., — 54.
  Acts, xvi. 31, — 162.
    xxvi., — 28.
  Romans, ii. 7, — 106.
  1 Corinthians, xiii., xv., — 28.
    xiii. 11, — 44.
  2 Corinthians, iii. 5, — 44.
  Ephesians, vi. 1, 4, 23, — 37.
  Colossians, iii. 20, 21, — 37.
    iv. 2, — 106.
  Hebrews, vi. 19, — 183.
  James, iv. — 28.
  2 Peter, iii. 18, — 18.
  Revelation, v. 6, — 28.
Shakespeare, quotations, 90, 106.
Shelley, quotation, 44.
Sidney, quotation, 44.

Signs, 207.
Silk-worm, an illustration, 27.
Soldiers in drill and battle, 47.
Spider eats double, an illustration, 58.
Spider's web, an illustration, 97.
Spurgeon, quotation, 144.
Supernatural influence, 178.
Superstition, 175.
Strawberry, an illustration, 25.
Sympathy, Philosophy of, 145.
Sympathetic teachers, 138.

Table-tipping, 179.
Telescope, an illustration, 84.
Temperance texts, 33.
Tempering steel, an illustration, 169.
Texts germinate thought, 26.
Tendency of pleasant emotions, 133.
Theatres, 140.
Thinking, Art of, 45.
Truth, application of, 26.
  harnessed to real life, 27.

Unbelief, 170.
Use of the Imagination, 121.

Verbal memory, 24.
Virtues not meritless, 114.

Webster, quotations, 106, 120.
Weeds, an illustration, 35.
Will, 205.
Will-sympathy, 148.
Wish, 215.

Young, quotations, 162, 282, 205.
Young people, tendency of, 31.

www.ingramcontent.com/pod-product-compliance
Lightning Source LLC
Chambersburg PA
CBHW021835230426
43669CB00008B/974